FOREWORD
EVELYN CHRISTENSON

HEART TO HEART WITH PASTORS' WIVES

TWELVE WOMEN
SHARE THE WISDOM
THEY'VE GAINED AS
PARTNERS IN MINISTRY

⸙

Sally Christon Conway
Colleen Townsend Evans
Joy P. Gage
Kathryn Stephens Grant
Anna Hayford
Pamela Hoover Heim
Catherine Hickem
Gail MacDonald
Anne Ortlund
Carol Rhoads
Mary Lou Whitlock

COMPILED BY
LYNNE DUGAN

Regal Books
A Division of Gospel Light
Ventura, California, U.S.A.

Published by Regal Books
A Division of Gospel Light
Ventura, California, U.S.A.
Printed in U.S.A.

Regal Books is a ministry of Gospel Light, an evangelical Christian publisher dedicated to serving the local church. We believe God's vision for Gospel Light is to provide church leaders with biblical, user-friendly materials that will help them evangelize, disciple and minister to children, youth and families.

It is our prayer that this Regal Book will help you discover biblical truth for your own life and help you meet the needs of others. May God richly bless you.

For a free catalog of resources from Regal Books/Gospel Light please contact your Christian supplier or call 1-800-4-GOSPEL.

Library of Congress Cataloging-in-Publication Data
Heart to heart with pastor's wives : twelve pastors' wives open their hearts to share
   the wisdom gained as partners in the pastorate / compiled by Lynne Dugan.
        p.   cm.
     ISBN 0-8307-1648-3
     1. Clergymen's wives—United States—Religious life. 2. Evangelicalism—
United States.   I. Dugan, Lynne.
     BV4395.H326   1994   94-6685
     253'.2—dc20   CIP

1 2 3 4 5 6 7 8 9 10 11 12 13 14 15 16 / 02 01 00 99 98 97 96 95 94

Rights for publishing this book in other languages are contracted by Gospel Literature International (GLINT). GLINT also provides technical help for the adaptation, translation and publishing of Bible study resources and books in scores of languages worldwide. For further information, contact GLINT, P.O. Box 4060, Ontario, CA 91761-1003, U.S.A., or the publisher.

To the Author and Finisher of our faith, the Lord Jesus Christ, who "will accomplish what concerns me" (Ps. 138.8, *NASB*). To my beloved husband, Bob, my closest friend for more than 40 years in marriage and ministry, who suggested I create a survey to determine the needs of pastors' wives. To our stalwart son, Bob III, his wonderful wife, Alisa, our grandson, Robby IV, and to our darling daughter, Cheri. To my friends who contributed to this book out of their experiences in pastoral ministry. To the National Association of Evangelical Women's Commission, who caught the vision of Support Groups for Pastors' Wives. To Brenda Josee, who encouraged me for more than four years to produce this book. Ultimately, to pastors' wives and women in ministry— choice, but often unsung, servants of God.

CONTENTS

APPENDICES

oreword

Evelyn Christenson

EVELYN CHRISTENSON WAS A PASTOR'S WIFE FOR 18 YEARS, DURING WHICH TIME
she taught and lectured in the United States and Canada. She has
received several honors, including "Churchwoman of the Year" by
the Religious Heritage of America. She has been listed in several edi-
tions of Who's Who in the Midwest _and_ Who's Who of American
Women _as well as in other directories. She has been active in more_
than 10 Christian organizations, as well as holding key positions in
many others, including several prayer groups. Evelyn became the

founding president of the United Prayer Ministries in 1973, based in Minnesota, and has been chairperson of the board since 1976. She is the author of several best-selling books, including What Happens When Women Pray *(awarded Platinum Book Award from Evangelical Christian Publishers Association [ECPA]) and* Lord, Change Me! *(Gold Book Award from ECPA). Evelyn and her husband, Harold, have three children and seven grandchildren. They live in St. Paul, Minnesota.*

When I became a pastor's wife more than 40 years ago, how I longed for advice and someone to tell me what to say and do. But virtually nothing was written in those days to guide me into that scary world of the unknown. Evidently, it never dawned on anybody that moving into "the parsonage" would not be enough to fill all the pastor's wife's dreams and needs. That she needed training, understanding and a support group just for her was unheard of.

But that is not true anymore. These needs are being addressed openly; and now God has deeply burdened Lynne Dugan, herself a former's pastor's wife, to write about and to do something about these needs. The result is this book—a book that not only identifies problems common to most pastors' wives, but also gives specific, practical biblical answers to them.

As I read this manuscript, how I wished I had had this information 40 years ago. And how it confirmed what I have struggled, mostly alone, to find out for myself. How I wished Lynne had brought together these 11 godly, highly esteemed pastors' wives with all of their expertise gleaned from their collective years as "the pastor's wife." How skillfully and sensitively they have handled biblical unity, not only in calling, but in an intimate sex life, as well as infidelity within the ministry. Such great wisdom they have shared on pastors' kids in their fishbowl existence and the parents' relationships to those kids. How I could have used that!

It was thrilling for me to read the instruction to today's pastor's wife for the necessity of "self-feeding" from the Bible; which through many years of practice became the most important part of my life as a Christian woman. And their understanding of, and hope in, midlife crisis and menopause! And stress! And abuse in the Christian home! Then there was their encouraging know-how and results of discipling and mentoring others. And the fantastic chapter showing that, although people say 65 is the end of all productivity, God is not through with the dedicated, matured, still vigorous pastor's wife in her retirement. And that beautiful chapter on commitment to and dependence first on God Himself and then to His work wonderfully summed up the goal of the pastor's wife.

But one of the most exciting parts of this book is the unique solution to the loneliness so many pastors' wives experience—support groups within their own profession. When Lynne's interviews and her survey of Christian women produced the indisputable fact that wives of pastors need companionship among women in like ministry, she began organizing these support groups in our nation's capital. Now she is spawning these groups nationwide through the Women's Commission of the National Association of Evangelicals. In *Heart to Heart with Pastors' Wives*, Lynne includes valuable "how-to" information for forming and maintaining these support groups across denominational lines, in independent fellowships and in seminaries.

God is doing an incredible thing these days. He is breaking down centuries-old barriers of denominations, races and Christian organizations to form the biblical unity of Christ's Body. And I believe bringing the pastors' wives together across these lines is one of the greatest ways God is accomplishing His purpose for today. And God knew all along that it would be one of His best ways of solving the age-old problems of loneliness, prayer support and mutual understanding faced by pastors' wives.

Pastors' wives: those super moms, super wives, super hostesses, lovers and partners of the men God called to fill the pulpits of His churches!

What an incredible book. Here it is, dear pastor's wife, for you today.

rom an Open Heart

Lynne Dugan

LYNNE DUGAN IS FOUNDER AND PRESIDENT OF THE WASHINGTON DC METRO Association of Evangelical Pastors' Wives, which has grown into a national ministry of Support Groups for Pastors' Wives. She works in the National Association of Evangelicals' (NAE) Washington office, where she is the first person visitors meet, whether by phone or by elevator to the office three blocks from the White House. She serves on the advisory board of the NAE Women's Commission, which sponsors this national outreach to pastors' wives.

*In 1990, she wrote and helped implement the nationwide NAE
Survey of Pastors' Wives, and as a result began to compile* Heart to
Heart with Pastors' Wives. *Lynne was a minister's wife in New Jersey,
New Hampshire, Illinois and Colorado for 18 years, before her hus-
band, Bob, became the Director of the NAE Office of Public Affairs
in 1978. She is a graduate of Nyack College (New York), attended
Wheaton College (Illinois) and earned a B.A. from National-Louis
University (Illinois).*

In 1991, she was included in Who's Who in American Universities and Colleges, *and was recognized as Alumna of the Year for Service to Society by Nyack College in 1985. Lynne has been active in
several political campaigns and has coordinated and taught seminars and Bible studies in political, church, educational and community circles. The Dugans have two children and one grandchild.
They live in Vienna, Virginia.*

Serving in the Ministry

I love to surprise people; so before leaving for college I visited Mrs.
Cutts, who was my piano teacher from third grade through junior
high. She could hardly wait for an answer: Did I still want to be a
missionary, or marry a minister? She remembered I had told her
about my dream to either go to the mission field or to serve in
church work. She knew I became a believer when I was 13 years old
at a Bible conference, and had dedicated my life to serve God "full
time." I guess Mrs. Cutts thought these were pretty high expectations for a young girl.

Because I wanted to prepare for ministry, I chose courses in
high school and college that I thought would help me in the ministry.
I also believed that if it was the Lord's will for me to marry, He
would lead me to the right man. While I was attending college I was
dating a fine Christian businessman. Most everybody thought we

would get married, and it was a real struggle for me. But during revival meetings at college, God reminded me of my original call to ministry and I determined if I were to marry, it would be someone who had the same vision.

Fortunately, when I transferred to another college, I met a tall, dark, handsome man, Bob Dugan, who loved the Lord and was preparing for a pastoral ministry. We fell in love. After we were married that August, we took a three-week, 5,000-mile honeymoon trip from New Jersey to Maine via the Canadian Rockies, then to Southern California where Bob would attend seminary and I would work at a local bank to help "put hubby through."

That first year we loved working together on weekends as high school sponsors in a nearby church. Then the next year Bob was invited to be the youth pastor in a neighboring church where I joined him in ministry with the young people. Bob and I knew we would be a harmonious team in our idealized version of our own nearly perfect church, my vocal ministry complementing his preaching.

On the last day of 1958, we were preparing to serve in our first church. Here came the moving van pulling up in front of our New England parsonage. It did not take us long to realize the only professional mover was the driver. His hired men were rounded up from the town square where they had already celebrated New Year's Eve that morning. We enjoyed a good laugh when we discovered the garden tools in the upstairs bathroom. It was like standing on the set of a Laurel and Hardy movie!

But it was not long before the laughter stopped. Bob was the only pastor for a congregation of 300 people, so he was busy every day and evening. I took care of our two preschool children, taught the college Sunday School class, worked in Pioneer Girls, did visitation, was a soloist and choir member. We loved to have people in our home, so we kept the door open for group gatherings. Whenever a need was presented to me, I felt obligated to fill the gap. Needless to say, my husband and I were too busy most of the time to know what the other one was doing; not exactly teamwork as we had planned in seminary. And we were too tired to build and renew our relationship with each other.

Stop the Treadmill

I was married to a minister, but I sensed a calling to the pastoral ministry just as strongly as my husband did. I wanted to serve faithfully, but slowly I began feeling like an unpaid assistant pastor. I used to sing, "Let me burn out for You dear Lord, burn and wear out for You," and I almost did!

I felt as if I were on a treadmill and could not reach the stop button. Suddenly, one cold winter morning I found myself pounding my pillow saying, "I can't stand it anymore! I can't stand it anymore!" My sleepy husband did not have the foggiest notion of what was wrong with me.

I was desperate enough to *really* unload my feelings. I felt guilty sharing how I felt, because my husband was so busy and burdened with other people's problems. I did not want to add to his already heavy load. The built-up resentment and anger flowed out that morning. Bob listened sympathetically. Before long, he had an idea that was as effective as the stop button on a treadmill. He would take one day off every week to be with me and our children—52 weeks a year.

We agreed to serve our first congregation for the princely sum of $70 a week plus the parsonage and oil for its furnace. We have never known any other ski area to do this, but New Hampshire's Gunstock provided free season tickets for pastors and their families. We took up skiing with a vengeance, discovering a whole new outlook on winter, as well as family life. Every Tuesday I gladly traded the treadmill for a pair of skis!

Our experience helped Bob and me to empathize with the needs of other pastors and their families. During our next pastorate in Illinois, Bob conducted an anonymous survey with a group of pastors. His last question to the pastors was: Do you think your wife would say that you give her and your children enough of your time? Only 1 out of 38 pastors answered yes; it was Bob. I was able to confirm his answer, and we both felt sorry for the other 37 wives. To some degree, most must have resented the Lord, their church or their husband. Incidentally, we left the meeting early to play 18 holes of golf together.

A New Identity

In the late '60s, I experienced a freak accident in a dentist's chair that produced a locked jaw for four months, and I was not able to sing anymore. My head ached unbearably when I tried to sing and my throat was constricted. To this day, that condition has not changed.

I did not realize until the accident how much my identity was tightly wrapped around my performance as a singer. Being unable to sing anymore made me feel completely lost. Consequently, I doubled my efforts by performing other ministries. I was teaching three Bible studies, instead of one, to make up for the one lost talent.

I realized my identity did not depend on people's opinions of me or my frenetic church work, but rather on my being a child of God. He loved me for myself

Finally, in extreme frustration, I blurted out: "I just can't please everyone. I feel like a yo-yo; up when I'm pleasing people, and down when I'm not."

Bob responded, "Honey, just be yourself."

I protested. "But I don't know who I am. I don't know how to be myself."

Because I knew my life needed to be sorted out, I spent more time in the Word. Isaiah said it for me: "Woe is me, for I am undone!" (Isa. 6:5). I prayed God would touch me as He did the needy prophet and He did. I felt a burden lift when I realized what I knew all along. My identity did not depend on people's opinions of me or my frenetic church work, but rather on my being a child of God. He loved me for myself.

I asked God to forgive, cleanse and fill me with His Spirit. I knew I did not have to prove my worth to Him anymore or try to please everyone; just try to please Him. The Lord became my top priority. I could now hand over some of my added responsibilities to other qualified women in the congregation. Now I feel as if I wear an identification bracelet bearing the inscription "Child of God," and I am finally free to cut the yo-yo string.

Serving in the Nation's Capital

A few years after we were called to serve in a Colorado church, Bob dropped a bombshell. He said, "You know Honey, I've been thinking that I may not always be in the pastorate." I could not believe my ears. How would this affect all of us? I did not want to spoil his dream; I was a dreamer myself. What did he have in mind? "I'm not positive," he said, "but I think it may be politics." He had to be kidding! But he was not kidding; he was interested in running for Congress.

What did I do when my world was about to fall apart? I felt like a trapeze artist who just left her platform to swing to the waiting bar suspended in space. For many days I suffered in silence, wanting to keep peace at any cost in my family. I wondered how I would fit into Bob's new career. Up till now we had worked "shoulder to shoulder" (Zeph. 3:9, NIV). Bob tried to assure me that he never intended to quit "the ministry" even if he were elected to Congress. But that was not a pattern that fit into my categories.

Suddenly, one day in my daily Bible reading, I understood. "And the government shall be upon His shoulder" (Isa. 9:6). I used to sing those words from Handel's Messiah, but never understood the full meaning until that point. I realized government is ultimately on God's shoulders, not ours. We have nothing to fear. Our King instituted government, not mankind. We are still to be active, responsible citizens, however, knowing that God is ultimately in control. I further read in Romans 13:6 (NIV) that political officeholders are called "God's servants," but are called "God's ministers" in the King James Version. Fascinating.

Several months later, having the children's and my blessing, Bob resigned from our church in order to run for Congress. I had finally grabbed the other trapeze bar, so to speak, and landed on Bob's political platform. Although being a Congressman was not to be, Bob won respect from his political party and his volunteers, but especially from our children, Bob III and Cheri—and me.

A New Ministry

In 1978, The National Association of Evangelicals asked Bob to become director of its Office of Public Affairs in Washington, D.C. As it turned out, the Lord wanted us in the nation's capital after all. A few years later we were a team again when Bob asked me to be the office receptionist.

Working for a national association gave me a sense of national ministry for women. But I was not focused on what group of women I should minister to or how to help until I shared my concern with Vonette Bright, cofounder of Campus Crusade for Christ, and Dee Jepsen, women's liaison to President Reagan. Together, they arranged a retreat with six other women who were in leadership.

During one of our retreat sessions, the facilitator asked, "What is your main burden for ministry? What group of people do you most want to help?" We isolated ourselves to meditate on the questions. I did not know, so I prayed God would reveal the answers. Certain Scriptures held my attention.

"That you also may have fellowship with us; and truly our fellowship is with the Father and with His Son Jesus Christ" (1 John 1:3).

"Consider one another in order to stir up love and good works" (Heb. 10:24).

"If therefore there is any encouragement in Christ,...consolation of love,...fellowship of the Spirit,...affection and compassion,...by being of the same mind, maintaining the same love, united in spirit, intent on one purpose" (Phil. 2:1,2, NASB).

I was not ready for my own answer; in fact, I was surprised. Slowly, I realized my concern centered around helping pastors' wives, but I thought it was strange because I was not in the pastoral ministry anymore. When the group gathered again, I was able to pinpoint my concern on pastors' wives but I had no ideas on how I could help them. Perhaps in some way I could encourage these women through a fellowship group.

In the '80s, I began to realize how many pastors' wives were hurting. As I crisscrossed the nation with Bob, meeting with various denominations, pastors' wives freely confided their problems to me. But I also had a personal reason for wanting to minister to other pastors' wives.

Overcoming Personal Problems

During his teens, unknown to us, our son began to drink. What a jolt it was when we frantically were calling around one Sunday at 5:00 A.M. to find the whereabouts of our son. That was the day we discovered how serious the problem was. We finally located our son in jail for disorderly conduct while under the influence of alcohol. We were crushed. Bob found someone else to preach the two services that morning, we picked up our remorseful son, and then Bob drove over to the church to submit his resignation. Fortunately, wiser heads prevailed.

We thought our son's drinking problem had been resolved with the Lord, especially when he was married, but it recurred and eventually led to the breakup of his marriage. This time I was the one who felt disqualified to minister.

As I was agonizing in prayer one day, the Lord showed me I was angry over the situation, but ultimately angry with God. I held on to the end, believing God would reconcile our son's and his wife's relationship to Him and to each other; but it did not happen, although I had "all faith, so as to remove mountains" (1 Cor. 13:2, *NASB*). The problem was not removed.

I knew God was all powerful, so why didn't He step in and fix everything? For some unknown reason He did not, and I had to accept the fact. I asked God to forgive my anger directed at Him, at my son and daughter-in-law, and especially myself. Eventually, I asked God to "bless the mess," praised Him and asked that this experience bring glory to His name so that other families in pastoral ministry could be helped.

For the record, those days are long behind us. Our son is happily married and living for the Lord. Of course, at that time the outcome was far from certain.

Conducting a National Survey

For several years, I laid the foundation by conducting focus groups. I interviewed pastors' wives and counselors of clergy. I read, conducted research and drew from my own 18 years in the ministry.

The ministry offers high hopes as well as hard realities. Our purpose in writing this book is to give reason for the hope and comfort in the realities.

From this research, I began developing a survey for pastors' wives. (See appendix 1 for the complete survey.)

The National Association of Evangelicals was the perfect organization to implement the survey of evangelical pastors' wives sponsored by the Women's Commission and the Task Force on the Family. My purpose was to detail the personal needs in areas of pastors' wives' resources, roles, spiritual life, family problems, life issues, information about their church, children and careers.

The Purpose of This Book

Nobody understands a pastor's wife better than another pastor's wife. That is why I invited 11 qualified women who are my friends, and who have a wealth of experience as pastors' wives, to write a chapter for this book. Their subjects were chosen to respond to the vital interests of the pastors' wives who took the survey. Each contributor brings her insight from her own experience and spiritual wisdom, and is acknowledged as a woman of excellence by her own peers.

It is my dream that in helping pastors' wives, renewal will come to their families. Healthy and happy pastoral families can strengthen a church's influence.

The ministry offers high hopes as well as hard realities. Our purpose in writing this book is to give reason for the hope and comfort in the realities. It is my prayer that all who read this book will be encouraged to serve the Lord with gladness, and be assured of God's love as they minister to the Lord, to their families and to others who need their love.

CHAPTER TWO

Husband and Wife: A Union Designed by God

Colleen Townsend Evans

COLLEEN TOWNSEND EVANS WAS UNDER CONTRACT FOR SEVERAL YEARS AS AN actress with Twentieth Century Fox Studios when she was a teenager; she also attended Brigham Young University in Utah. In 1987, she was chair of the Greater Washington Billy Graham Crusade, and in the same year, The Religious Heritage of America named her Church-woman of the Year. Colleen is a corporator of Covenant Life Insurance Company, is a member of the board of directors of World Vision, U.S., is now serving as renewal associate of Presbyterians for Renewal and

also serves on the advisory board of Evangelicals for Social Action.
Colleen is the author of nine books, including A Deeper Joy *and* Make Me Like You, Lord. *With her husband, Louis, she is coauthor of a book on marriage entitled,* Bold Commitment. *The Evanses have ministered in churches for more than 41 years, including 18 years at the National Presbyterian Church in Washington, D.C. They are now serving at the Menlo Park Presbyterian Church in Menlo Park, California, where Louis is part-time pastor-at-large. Colleen and her husband have four children and four grandchildren. They live in Redwood City, California.*

When God created us male and female, I think God smiled. His good design of partnership between one man and one woman for life provided the way for intimacy and ecstasy, as well as the ultimate human means of knowing one another. The "knowing" comes by a process—a lifelong journey of self-disclosure we call communication. Communication takes place in many ways: by word (though some studies show that only 7 percent of what we communicate is verbal), tone of voice (38 percent), facial and body language (55 percent). So even without opening our mouths we are constantly communicating, and always involved in the process.

One of the deepest, most profound means of communication is the physical intimacy and sexual union God has designed for partners in marriage. It is a unique and beautiful expression of love. It is not sex as seen in the media or reflected in the attitude of our society. That kind of cultural hype would have us believe that *eroticism* and *love* are synonymous, and those of us who have made "until death do us part" promises know this is not true. The pressures of childbearing, rearing a family, empty nesting, as well as the challenge of making ends meet and creating quality moments in the crunch of busy schedules require far more than physical gratification. They call for a committed partnership of body, mind and spirit. Sex alone will never be enough to see us through.

Having said that, however, I want to say that sex *is* incredibly important; it is far more important, in my opinion, than many Christians are willing to concede. There is far too much talk about sex *outside* of marriage, and not nearly enough about the deep pleasure, the adventure and the ministry of sex *within* marriage. And it is *this* kind of godly sexual union on which I want to focus.

The Biblical Base for Sexuality

Sisters, sex is good—*very* good—because it *comes* from God. God dreamed it, and brought it into being. It was our loving and imaginative God who made us sexual beings; He created the human body to be fascinating, to be desired and shared with one covenant partner for life. This is powerful stuff! Sex between married partners is good because God created it, and us, for each other. In this context then, "sex is not dirty; it is holy ground"; it is the nurturing soil in which great love can grow. So as you and your spouse come together in lovemaking, remember that, believe it and celebrate the joy!

Of course, sex is only part of our total life, but it serves a double purpose as it both *creates* union and *reflects* it.

My friend Dr. Fran Davis, a gifted marriage counselor and family therapist, says:

A couple's sexual relationship is the arena in which their
        whole life is played out—
                their honesty,
                        vulnerability
                                openness
                                        lack of withholding
                                                their playfulness
                                                        their "power-games."

I think what my friend says contains more than an element of truth. As I look back over the years of my attitude about my marriage as a whole, it has often been reflected in my attitude toward our sexual relationship.

So if God created sexual intimacy to be beautiful and good, how can we as pastor/spouse couples better experience this goodness in our lives? Even as I write, I realize how impossible, even arrogant, it

God calls us to union, not fusion!

is to think that I might be able to answer that question in these few lines. Besides, I do not have an "answer" as such—only ideas born out of my life in Christ, and my more than 40 years of marriage to Louie. Here are some of my convictions, not in order of their importance, but simply as they come to mind.

Differentiation

An important prerequisite for a mutually fulfilling sexual give-and-take is a clear sense of differentiation between partners. Many of us "religious types" have bought into the myth that says when two become one (see Mark 10:6-9) individuality must be sacrificed. But I think when that happens, it works against union. God calls us to *union,* not fusion!

I have a dear friend who has worked long and hard to move from a place of fusion, where she felt she was only an extension of her pastor-husband, to the place where she now is "a woman, married to a minister." As a result of her journey, she now feels united with her husband in a "true covenant partnership."

Perhaps, because I did not grow up in the church, having the traditional pastor's wife model in mind, I have never felt pressured to "live the role." Shirley Hartley, a sociologist, writes that mainline protestant clergy wives are probably the most extreme example of the traditional female role in our society, "with expectations tha⁺ indi viduals in that role will subordinate their own interests to husbands, church and parishioners as well."[1]

Having come to faith in Christ as an adult, I have felt I was first and foremost a *woman* in Christ, with a clear understanding that my commitment meant serving Christ in some way all the days of my life; second, I was a Christian woman married to a Christian man; and finally, a Christian woman with my own sense of call, married to a Christian man who had a call from God to do pastoral ministry.

When Louie and I got married, we really felt we were linking arms to do ministry together. This sequence may seem insignificant, but I believe it has helped us feel a sense of healthy differentiation that in turn has enhanced our sense of one-fleshness in our marriage. I *do* believe that part of the mystery and beauty of union is that two very different people can come together as one, each partner clearly their "own person" before God, yet totally committed to the partnership. This kind of marriage is not an institutional stranglehold but a covenant promise, a voluntary embrace in which mutually fulfilling sex can be a growing reality.

Faithfulness

Emil Brunner wrote, "Marriage is built not so much on love as on fidelity." But for me, love and fidelity need to walk hand in hand. Surely someone experiencing "true love" cares so much about the other person that the physical expressions of love become the private and exclusive sanctuary of life together. Of course, I am speaking ideally as I believe God intends our relationship to be. We all know, however, that life does not always fall into simple, straight, ideal lines.

Perhaps at this point we should detour a moment to mention, but not dwell on the fact, that Christian couples, and clergy couples specifically, are not immune to breaches of fidelity. In our society, where intimacy is valued, but so rarely achieved, our pastor-husbands who are sensitive, caring and genuinely interested in parishioners can find their human warmth and godly compassion easily misunderstood.[2]

Many people are needy, and ministers, as well as doctors, therapists and other "helper-type" professionals are vulnerable targets. Pastors are peculiarly susceptible, because spiritual bonding and intellectual stimulus are added to the relational dynamics common to all the helping professions. An authoritative power also goes with these positions, and more than a few caregivers fall into the temptation to misuse that power. The result, as the Christian community knows too well, is sad and heartbreaking for everyone concerned.[3]

Of course, the good news of Christ's gospel is that when anyone falls from faithful living and truly repents, grace and forgiveness abound. And God can heal all the broken hearts when He is given all the pieces. But that is another chapter for another book someday.

Returning to our original theme of *union as God designed it*, I want to underscore the ideal, which is the call of God to *both* partners to live faithfully with one another "till death do them part."

Louie and I always have believed that Jesus taught a kind of radical, transparent fidelity when He said: "I say to you, that everyone who looks on a woman to lust for her has committed adultery with her already in his heart" (Matt. 5:28, *NASB*). (Likewise, every woman who looks lustfully on a man.)

This verse implies *mental* as well as *physical* faithfulness. Jesus was so wise! He knew that the first line of defense against breaking our covenant promises was not in the erogenous zones of the body but right between the ears where our mind and imagination reside. He also knew that fidelity would provide the solid spiritual and psychological base intimacy would need to survive and flourish. I know it is true for me. Without a faithful husband, I would struggle to feel secure enough to respond, or initiate sexually with my whole being. (And I feel certain God does not want us to be halfhearted lovers.) But within the safety of a true commitment, I can enjoy a kind of abandon that is astonishing, even to me.

Marriage: God's Visible Expression of His Covenant with Us

I think we as Christian couples can experience the goodness of our sexuality when we understand and believe that our union symbolizes the real nature of what our relationship with God is meant to be. Scripture clearly likens our life in Christ to our life together as married partners. The Old Testament alludes to it. In the New Testament, Paul makes a strong connection.

Submit to One Another Out of Reverence for Christ

> Wives, submit to your husbands *as to the Lord.* Husbands, love your wives, just *as Christ loved the church and gave himself up for her* (Eph. 5:22,25, *NIV,* italics added).

Jesus lived this out on the cross. As well, the words the Bible uses to describe physical union between husband and wife, "to

May we never consider the physical intimacies we enjoy in marriage as a separate category from our lives in Christ. The two are inseparably intertwined.

know" (see Luke 1:34), are the very ones used to describe the intimate way we can know God, through Christ. So the uniting of two people who make a lifetime covenant is a visible expression of God's covenant with us.[4]

May we never consider the physical intimacies we enjoy in marriage as a separate category from our lives in Christ. The two are inseparably intertwined. The way we love and minister to our spouse, with our *whole* being, is every bit as spiritual as anything we will ever do in the church.

Closing Thoughts

I would like to close with some thoughts a beautiful sister, Pat Grant, wrote and shared with me some years ago.[5] For me, she has said all that needs to be said on this subject.

Within Christian marriage—
Sex is beautiful, delightful, necessary; God made it so.
It is an expression of oneness...
                a total commitment...
                a complete self-giving...
                a sacred obligation.
Sex is a privilege—
                not a right—to claim selfishly
                not a favor—to withhold selfishly
                not a weapon—to dominate another
                not a reward—for good behavior
Each one finds fulfillment in satisfying the other.
        The body does not belong to its owner—but to the partner—
        to be enjoyed fully—cherished attentively—and loved unselfishly.

Amen!
In my opinion, this kind of sexual union fulfills the good design of creation and makes God smile. At the same time, it provides a solid foundation from which we and our pastor-husbands can reach out in ministry to serve our needy and broken world, in the name of Christ.
        Sisters, let's live up to our privilege.

Notes
1. Shirley F. Hartley, "Marital Satisfaction Among Clergy Wives," *Review of Religious Research* 19 (1978): 178.

2. For a more in-depth study of caretakers' vulnerability, see "Faith, Hope, and the 'Urge to Merge' in Pastoral Ministry" by J. Steven Muse, Ph.D. in *The Journal of Pastoral Care* 46 (Fall 1992): 3.

3. Ibid.

4. For an expanded look at the link between our union with God and union in marriage read Mike Mason's excellent book *The Mystery of Marriage: As Iron Sharpens Iron* (Sisters, OR: Multnomah Books, 1985).

5. Pat Grant has taught sex education in the Washington, D.C. schools. She is a social worker with Family and Child Services, a private agency.

lergy Kids:
Give Them a Break

Catherine Hickem

CATHERINE HICKEM IS A PSYCHOTHERAPIST AND HAS BEEN IN PRIVATE PRACTICE since 1990. She conducts workshops, seminars and retreats, and has had extensive experience in working as a marriage and family therapist. She graduated Magna Cum Laude with a master of science degree in social work from the University of Louisville in Louisville, Kentucky. She was honored as one of the Outstanding Young Women of America in 1983. She has written monthly features for Contempo, a periodical of the Woman's Missionary Union; she wrote "PK: Bless-

ing or Burden?" for Quarterly Review, *January 1986, and was a contributing author of* Minister's Mate: Two for the Price of One? *Catherine and her husband, Neil, minister at First Baptist Church of Delray Beach, Florida, and have been in the ministry for 16 years. The Hickems have two children.*

∾✦∾

Perspective

Some time ago, I was telling a story to a group of children at church. I began to describe a person who had disobeyed, had been swallowed by a fish and was spit out several days later. I asked the children to tell me the name of the person I had just described. Hands went up all over the room. One little three-year-old girl raised her hand and waved it excitedly. Surprised that she might know the answer, I called on her.

"Brenda, what was that person's name?"

Using all the gusto she possessed, she yelled, "Pinocchio!"

Probably most of you were thinking, as I was, that she would say Jonah. It never dawned on me that Pinocchio had similar characteristics to Jonah. But that experience taught me something of great importance: Perspective is everything, and there is always more than one view to consider.

Such is the case with clergy kids. They are fortunate to be exposed to some of the greatest riches under heaven, as well as the deepest pain on earth. They are children who have been selected by God to experience His work from a unique position. Thus, as their parents, we have been granted the awesome task of helping our children see and experience God through sometimes seemingly empty religion and human dysfunction.

As a psychotherapist, I have been fortunate to share the lives of many wonderful people, some of whom were clergy families. They were brought to my office for various reasons, but they all had one thing in common: emotional pain. As we waded through their hurt and pain, I began to see the disappointment and rejection that was created from unmet expectations.

I have never been fond of expectations, because they only seem to create unnecessary problems. So it is with clergy kids. They often find themselves caught in a vise between their parents' expectations and those of the church members. As a result, clergy kids are set up to fail.

The purpose of childhood is to explore all the wonder, fascination and joy that life has to offer. Growing, learning and experiencing life in a safe and loving way will draw children toward a healthy sense of self-worth and a tender relationship with God.

When clergy parents place unrealistic expectations on their kids, they place incredible pressure on them. This is often interpreted by the children as conditional love from their parents. If children feel and believe that they can never make their parents happy, they will do one of two things. They will quit trying and rebel, or they will develop such a sense of perfectionism that they will never be content or truly happy.

Forgiveness

A certain minister had a daughter who was in her 20s. She was a lovely, compassionate woman who became pregnant during her junior year of college. She chose to keep the baby, as abortion or adoption were not options for her. She returned home to live with her parents until the baby was born and her education was complete.

Several months after the baby's birth the young woman attended a service at a church where her father was the interim preacher. This minister-father was distant and cold toward his infant granddaughter and would have little to do with the baby. Several church members noticed his coldhearted reaction, and his witness to them was hurt. He demonstrated no mercy or grace. He was embarrassed that his daughter had fallen off her pedestal.

All parents would be disappointed if this same scenario happened to them. Feelings of disappointment, hurt, anger and sadness would all be normal in this situation. However, we cannot get stuck

It is important that our self-worth not be tied to our children's behavior. If my son or daughter misbehaves, it does not mean I am a bad person or a bad parent.

in our feelings and use them to harbor resentment. Forgiveness must be a necessary part of our lives if the Holy Spirit is to dwell within us.

Self-Worth

It is important that our self-worth not be tied to our children's behavior. If my son or daughter misbehaves, it does not mean I am a bad person or a bad parent. Nor does it mean that my children are bad. It simply means that as a parent I have been given another opportunity to teach my child a valuable lesson in consequences and benefits.

One time I was sitting in the choir, waiting for our musical to begin. My pastor-husband was welcoming the visitors and members. As I looked down to the second pew, all I could see were these two little feet dangling in the air. My son, Taylor, who was four years old at the time, had decided to try out his gymnastic skills, and what better place to do so than the front of the church. Several people in the choir and congregation were obviously amused at this event.

I came down from the choir and sat with Taylor until my husband was able to sit with him. I explained to Taylor why his behavior was not acceptable and told him how I wanted him to act. I was not angry or embarrassed. I should not expect a four-year-old child to have self-control in every situation. This was one of those times when he needed help.

Nothing can tap into our heart, pride and ego as can issues concerning our children. Our greatest highs and our lowest lows often come because of our children. We invest so much and whether we care to admit it or not, we expect something in return. In his book *The Hurried Child*, David Elkind states:

> They [children] are ready-at-hand targets for projecting unfulfilled needs, feelings, and emotions.[1]

Most of us would never knowingly harm our children. Yet, when we struggle to allow our children to be free of our unfinished business, we are perpetuating a cycle of generational sin.

I am a child of a pastor as is my husband, Neil. Having grown up in ministry-oriented families, we both understood the blessings and burdens our children would be born into. One of the greatest desires we had for our children was that they would grow up being treated as "normal" children by us as well as by those people who would be significant in their lives.

For other people to treat my children with respect, they must see their parents demonstrate it toward them first. It is our job to love, guide and discipline them with a sense of joy and commitment. Children learn to respect themselves as well as others if it is first demonstrated toward them.

Respecting our children sometimes means making difficult choices on their behalf. When my son, Taylor, was five months old, I discovered I was pregnant. I know what you are thinking. But you see, Taylor is adopted. Neil and I were more surprised than anyone when I discovered I was pregnant with Tiffany.

As a result, I had two babies at the same time. We had many long nights and hard days. Both babies were very ill in those first several years, especially Taylor. I had to miss a lot of church.

I was not as active as some people would have liked for me to be. But it was okay that I made my children a priority. Unlike many other couples, my husband and I could not alternate services and activities. Because he was the pastor, I always got elected to stay home with the kids.

People Pleasers

It is all right if we do not please everyone with our parenting decisions. We can never make everyone happy. We are going to make mistakes and we are entitled to make them. God teaches us many things through the errors of our ways. We can also use our mistakes to create a closer relationship with our children.

Because we are Christians, we often expect that church members are going to live up to their heavenly heritage. But as we all know, this is sometimes not the case. Thus, when our children become the object of criticism from people within the church, it is our job to respond with clear boundaries and a right heart.

After leading a conference for clergy wives, a woman came up to me and shared a true but painful story. She told me that one Wednesday night during a church business meeting, a member of her church brought up her children's behavior for discussion under the heading of "new business." This clergy wife picked herself up off the floor, stood up and addressed the issue.

First, the clergy wife asked her children to leave the auditorium. She did not want to subject them to any further embarrassment. She then addressed the congregation. She told them that her children were not "church business" and they would not be discussed in a public arena. She told the church member that if he had a problem with her kids, he would have to deal with her privately. She sat down, and the humiliating experience ended.

Not only was her children's behavior not church business; it was not anyone else's business either. I supported her courage to do what was right by her children. Often clergy parents will not address church members who inappropriately overstep boundaries. They will allow their children to be scapegoats, fearful they might hurt the church member's feelings. God has given us the responsibility to protect our children. If we do not protect them, then who will? I am not talking about being a defensive parent who believes his or her child can do no wrong. I am referring to people who have difficulty minding their own business and may have some spiritual problems with pride and authority.

When Taylor was almost two years old and Tiffany was nine months old, we were invited to a senior-adult pool party. Neil and I were in the pool playing with our little ones. A man who had been passively angry with Neil got into the pool with us. A few minutes later, the man began to push large waves of water onto Taylor's face. Taylor began to choke because he had taken in so much water. My husband handled the problem immediately, but I will tell you I was not a happy camper.

"Normal Life"

It is all right for people to be angry. The Bible says to be angry and sin not. It is not all right for church members who are upset with you or your spouse to take it out on your children. You and your spouse chose to go into ministry; your children did not. As adults, you have the ability to process and understand the dynamics of people and church personalities. Your children, however, are simply trying to find their way through childhood and adolescence.

I have heard of clergy kids being spanked, scolded, abused, rejected, publicly ridiculed and criticized by church members. As a child, I remember, on a few occasions, being inappropriately chastised and rejected because of people's inability to confront their anger with my dad. Thankfully, I have also experienced, as well as seen, the many blessings God has shed upon clergy kids through the love, compassion and understanding of godly people.

When the occasion has required it, I have told people that I do not want my children to be treated special or different. I simply want them to be treated as kids. Having a psychotherapist as a mom and a pastor for a dad, our kids have struggled to have a "normal life." Because of what we do in our professions, our kids are supposed to have it all together. Right? Wrong! The Hickem

Probably the greatest gift we can give our children is a genuine relationship with Jesus Christ and a home that is a harbor of happiness, safety and communication.

family is not exempt from sin, weaknesses, inadequacies or problems. We try to practice what we preach. However, we struggle like the rest of the population.

Clergy parents, like all other parents, have no guarantees that their children will be successful, happy and Christlike. Oftentimes it is assumed that if people are doing work for God, they can leave other responsibilities of their lives to God: That is not true.

We must remember that our children learn the nature of God based upon their relationship with us. If we are critical and judgmental, they will view God as being the same. If we are unconditionally loving, fair and patient, they will see God in a similar way. When I consider that reality, I am overwhelmed until I remember God is sufficient when I am not. I must ask for His guidance and direction.

Probably the greatest gift we can give our children is a genuine relationship with Jesus Christ and a home that is a harbor of happiness, safety and communication.

Parents' Hypocrisy

Several years ago I conducted research on clergy kids. The age of the respondents ranged from 8 to 81. One of the top criticisms by clergy kids across all ages and all ministerial roles (pastor, chaplain, music minister, etc.) was the discrepancy between the parents' public personality and their private one.

The data I collected told story after story about parents who were always hospitable, warm and friendly to church members, although a few minutes earlier those same parents had been berating each other and/or their children. This type of hypocrisy leads to a lack of parental respect, low self-worth and possibly rebellion.

When parents are hypocritical, they are acting outside their typical personality style all together. They may be attentive, say all the right things and be unconditionally accepting of others. When in their own homes, however, they are intolerant and impatient. They are almost like Dr. Jekyll and Mr. Hyde.

Children know when their parents are having a bad day and when their temperament is a regular lifestyle. We all have moments when we put on our "best face." The questions we have to ask ourselves are, "Do we have more bad days with our children than good?" "Do we treat other people better than the people to whom we are the most responsible?"

Asking forgiveness from our children is a nurturing experience for all of us. First of all, the act of seeking forgiveness keeps me humble and broken before the Lord. Second, it allows my children to see my need for God's grace in my life. Third, my children will not be as likely to develop problems with authority figures if I do not have to be right all the time. Fourth, it teaches my children through example that forgiveness is something we all need, and saying "I'm sorry" is a sign of strength, not weakness.

As we travel through this journey called life, we have the wonderful opportunity to impart meaningful spiritual experiences to our children. It is one thing for our children to see how we act and talk at church; it is another thing for them to see us at home.

Create Ministry Opportunities for Children

Neil and I have always believed missions begin at home. We want our children to grow up with a concern for others. As a result, we have created opportunities for them to participate in ministry. When Hurricane Andrew hit southern Florida, we were grateful we were spared the devastation and loss. We live about 50 miles from where the worst of Andrew's damage occurred. Our children saw the television pictures of children who lost everything. Taylor and Tiffany wanted to do something to help the victims. While their dad was in Miami helping with the relief effort, we talked about what they could do.

Taylor, seven, and Tiffany, six, decided to collect food. They would go door-to-door. Taylor decided he would do the talking and Tiffany would pull the wagon to carry the goods. We spent the next several hours collecting food. I intervened, only to answer questions from curious adults. The children were so excited when we finished, they wanted to do it again.

I am sure all of you have created similar opportunities for your children. Do not underestimate the effect these meaningful experiences will have in their future lives. We are laying a foundation that God can build on.

The Element of Time

One theme that has been an undercurrent throughout this whole chapter is the element of time. If we could bottle time and sell it, it would be sold out within the first hour. Our children need our time, yet this is probably one of the greatest struggles we face as parents. Healthy relationships require time, because communication does not come in microwave containers. Trust and communication develop as parents and children discuss their thoughts, feelings and experiences.

Clergy families have a unique problem with time because so much of their lives is connected with the church. Their spiritual, social and professional lives are all tied up into one arena. Thus, our children often see their parents at church more often than they see us at home.

My daughter, Tiffany, had just received her first report card for the first grade. She was proud of it and could not wait to show it to her dad. It just so happened that it was a Wednesday and we were at the weekly fellowship supper at church. As we were sitting at the table, Tiffany said, "Mom, where is my report card? I want to go show it to Daddy before the traffic starts." Tiffany was saying to me that she knew if she did not get to her dad quickly, she would have to stand in line to show him her report card. It is true that usually many people want to talk to Neil on Sundays and Wednesdays. That experience reiterated to me the importance of being accessible to our children daily.

In our family, we all know that togetherness is a commitment. We try to go away for an overnight activity once every three months to do something special (not expensive). Neil and I try to each take a child and do something with just that child once a week, such as going out for ice cream or taking a walk on the beach. Our children really cherish that one-on-one time with their parents.

All people are busy. Yet we make time for those things that are a priority in our lives. God instituted the family before He instituted the Church. It is ever so important to please God and not man. Again, we must rely on God's wisdom and discernment.

Although the marital relationship has already been discussed in chapter 1, I would like to reaffirm the importance it has on the life of your children. Your marriage is the guidepost by which your children will establish their standards for their own marriage. Allow your children to see you encouraging each other as well as working through conflict together. Parents courting each other also teaches children that marital relationships have to be nurtured to grow.

Confidence in Our Children

In Gary Smalley's book *The Blessing* (NavPress, 1988), he discusses the need for parents to give honor to their children. We do that in a variety of ways; one being our ability to encourage and demonstrate confidence in our kids. Children learn confidence if they first see we have confidence in them. It is a process that requires time, patience and love.

Tiffany and I were traveling to a retreat I was leading. I had been invited to bring her along. They were planning to have child care, so we decided we would take a few extra days and make it a special mother-daughter vacation.

For an activity at the retreat, I needed a skein of yarn rolled into a ball. Tiffany was five years old, and I thought she might be able to help roll the yarn while we were traveling in the car. She started rolling the yarn but was unable to form a ball, which frustrated her. She continued to try but became impatient with herself. I told her she could put it down and try later if she wanted to. I also told her that I knew she could do anything she wanted to if she wanted to do it badly enough.

We continued to travel down the road, and a few minutes later Tiffany picked up the ball of yarn. I noticed she worked more patiently and stayed with that task for more than an hour, until she was finished. "Look, Mom! I did it! I knew I could do it." The look of confidence and pride beamed on her precious little face from ear to ear. What had started out as my confidence in her had become something even more significant: her own self-confidence.

Needs and Feelings

I love being with my kids, and I am sure you enjoy being with yours. We have children for such a short time and it is important for us to make the most of the time we have together. Evaluate whether you are presenting the values and priorities you want your children to take with them when they leave home. It is never too late to change directions.

Talk to your children about the needs they have in their lives. They are usually pretty honest if you have given them permission to feel their feelings without getting in trouble. Encourage them to be honest with their feelings toward you. Do not ask your children those questions if you feel you cannot handle their responses with maturity and compassion. It is also important that you try not to defend or explain yourself. The purpose of this exercise is to listen. It can be risky for some children to be open, so be supportive if they share.

Feelings are important in healthy parent-child relationships. I find this area to be the most difficult for Christian people to handle effectively. Feelings are not good or bad, right or wrong. They are simply feelings. Children are feeling-oriented people until they hang around some adults too long.

If we do not allow our children to have their own feelings when they are young, they will be more likely to rebel when they are older. Adolescence is tough under good conditions. We can make it easier, however, by having a relationship with them that is safe. Kids will talk. Teens will talk. You want to be sure you are one of the people to whom they will talk.

In our home, we have a few rules about communicating. Our children are always allowed to tell us how they feel. They may tell us they do not like us or that they are angry with us. However, they are not permitted to call anyone names or be disrespectful and rude.

We also try not to use the word "you" when we are talking about how we feel, (i.e., "I feel sad when people yell at me"). Anytime people use the word "you," they are usually judging, blaming or criticizing. When your children can tell you how they feel from the very depths of their being, you will greatly improve the possibilities of rearing emotionally healthy children.

Anxiety and Fears

Children whose parents have undergone a traumatic experience, such as forced termination from a job, need special attention during and after the crisis. Parents have likely been traumatized by the pain, hurt and fear that go along with forced termination. Yet, adults usually have acquired some coping skills to survive such a storm.

Children's anxiety and fears are magnified when their entire network of support is snatched from them suddenly. They do not have the cognitive ability to process all that has happened and they feel like helpless victims. Understand that they will need to work through this experience as much as you will.

If you find yourself feeling overly worried about your children's emotional and spiritual growth, do not hesitate to seek out the services of a wise Christian psychotherapist. God places various people in our lives for His glory and honor. I consider being a psychotherapist a calling from God. I view what I do as a healing ministry. It is also my deepest prayer that whatever is said and done in my practice will please God. Pray that God will lead you in the decision whether or not to consult a psychotherapist.

Children Who Have Special Needs

I would also like to briefly mention the unique problems that go with having a child with special needs. If you have a child who has a special problem, be it physical, educational or emotional, do what you need to do to address your child's needs. God understands perfectly well what you are facing. No one will understand your struggle, heartbreak, weariness or sadness unless they have been where you are now.

Blessings of a Minister's Home

Pastors' children are blessed to be born into ministry-oriented homes. They often have the joy of being married by their fathers. Baptism, ordination and communion are ordinances the children can share in a special way with their ministry-oriented parent.

Children from a minister's family often are afforded opportunities to experience God's work through other Christian leaders. I have heard many stories of how godly men and women influenced the lives of clergy kids.

Above all, give yourself fully to the Lord. Allow the Holy Spirit to indwell your life. You can give no greater gift to your children than to live empowered by God's love and grace.

Faithfully and consistently pray for your children. Satan often attacks our most vulnerable place, and for many of us that area is our children. Pray a hedge of protection around them daily and teach them God's Word. Remember, God selected these children for you to raise. God knew what He was doing when He put you all together as a family. Trust Him to know what is best for them.

At the beginning of this chapter, I told you a story about Jonah and Pinocchio; I stated that perspective is everything. A heavenly perspective with your children will make your earthly travels more meaningful and blessed.

Note
1. David Elkind, *The Hurried Child: Growing Up Too Fast Too Soon* (Reading, MA: Addison-Wesley, 1981), p. 29.

CHAPTER FOUR

Self-Feeding of Scripture:
The Number One Survival Tool

Joy P. Gage

JOY P. GAGE IS A GRADUATE OF BIOLA UNIVERSITY IN LA MIRADA, CALIFORNIA, and attended the Univeristy of California Berkeley for special studies in publishing. She is on the faculty of five writers' conferences and is on the advisory board of Mount Hermon Christian Conference Center in Mount Hermon, California. She has received several writing and author awards, including the 1992 Pacesetter Award, and has been a conference speaker for more than 10 years throughout the United States. She is also on the Women's Commission of the NAE.

Joy has written more than a dozen books, including Trusting God Through the Worst of Times, *coauthored with her husband, Ken, as well as being a contributing author to several books, including* Still Moments *(a women's devotional). She has been a pastor's wife for more than 25 years. The Gages minister at Valley Baptist Church in San Rafael, California. They have three children and three grandchildren and live in San Rafael, California.*

The woman who becomes a minister's wife faces many unique challenges and learns very quickly that surviving life in the manse demands a strong personal commitment. She also discovers early on that she needs a great many people skills and a well-developed sense of humor.

Commitment keeps us hanging in there. People skills and a sense of humor equip us for the task. But after more than three decades in the parsonage, I have concluded that the number one survival tool is "self-feeding"—the ability to study the Scriptures on my own.

In the early years of our ministry, I read every book I could find for the pastor's wife. I discovered a half dozen techniques for dealing with difficult people. I learned how to turn a deaf ear to those who recited a list of the things my predecessor always did, and I picked up a few suggestions on how to avoid people who monopolized my time. It was all very practical information, but it left me feeling as though I was playing a game called "Keeping One Step Ahead of the Congregation." Somehow it was not enough. I needed a better reason to do what I assumed I was supposed to be doing.

I determined to find that reason in the Word. If God had a special standard for the woman in the manse, then I wanted to follow it.

Certain that I would never be adequate for the task, I embarked upon a personal study. Frantically, I searched the Scriptures in order to find everything that God expected of "me, the pastor's wife." It proved to be a short-lived study. I found very little that pertained to the role of a pastor's wife. But I found more than enough that pertained to the role of a believer.

Self-Feeding Required of All Believers

Long before I became a pastor's wife I memorized 1 Peter 2:2: "As newborn babes, desire the pure milk of the word, that you may grow thereby." It was in this challenge to all believers (not just to the pastor's wife or to Christian women) that I rediscovered the call to become a self-feeder.

Hindrances to Self-Feeding

Knowing what to do is not the same as knowing how to do it. Nor is knowing how to do it the same as doing it. Some women married to ministers have not been given the tools with which to develop a personal Bible study. They may be career women in their own right—highly skilled in their field. But the route to the manse did not include formal training in finding one's way around the Scriptures. The thought of developing a self-feeding program can be intimidating or overwhelming. Even women who have had some training find it difficult to begin such a program; I certainly did.

As a student at Biola University, I gained a solid foundation in biblical truth under such giants as Dr. J. Vernon McGee. After graduation, I served for a year under a home mission board where I taught children and adults under the watchful eye of my experienced coworker. My background should have given me the tools I needed for a structured time in the Word. But the truth is, I did not have the foggiest idea how to maintain a course of personal Bible study.

Two years after I graduated, I married Ken, a former Biola classmate, and I thought all my problems were solved. To put it bluntly, I expected Ken to take over where Dr. McGee had left off. Surely, my new husband would put structure into my Bible study efforts. He did, but not in the way I expected.

Ken took me to the Biola book room, suggested that I find something I wanted to study, announced that he would do the same and that we would discuss our findings together. My visions of sitting at his side and being spoon-fed for the rest of my life vanished in his arbitrary decision. It was not what I had expected. But it was the beginning of my self-feeding experience, working with a study guide and discussing my findings with another person.

Begin at the Beginning

Today, the woman who is beginning to develop her self-feeding skills has a wide selection of guides from which to choose. Most are designed to be used either individually or in a group. Some are topical, some are based on specific books of the Bible. The latter is a better choice if your ultimate aim is to develop self-feeding habits. By concentrating on a specific book, you will find it easier to ask, "What's this book all about?" Self-feeding skills develop as you list your own findings in response to the foregoing question.

Using a study guide is the logical place to start, but your long-term goal should be to be able to dig out truths without the aid of a study guide.

Acquire Tools for Bible Study

I took an important step in becoming a self-feeder when I began a study of a specific passage, using no other tools than my Bible and *Vine's Expository Dictionary of New Testament Words*. Ken had asked me to teach a one-hour class on Titus 2:3-5 to the women of our congregation. He handed me Vine's book, explained briefly how to use it and said, "I think you'll enjoy doing a word study on these verses." I felt as though a whole new world had been opened to me. From that point on, I began to seek out tools and techniques that would help me in my personal Bible study.

I highly recommend three basic tools: (1) *Vine's Complete Expository Dictionary of Old and New Testament Words* by W. E. Vine, Merrill F. Unger and William White Jr. (2) *Strong's Exhaustive Concordance of the Bible* by James Strong. This book will help you locate those elusive passages you can't find. But do not overlook the dictionaries in the back section: a "Hebrew and Chaldee Dictionary" for Old Testament words and a "Greek Dictionary of the New Testament." Fortunately, the need to know the biblical languages is eliminated through a system of numbered cross-references between the main concordance and the dictionary sections. (3) For an overview of each of the books of the Bible, I recommend Dr. J. Sidlow Baxter's *Exploring the Book.* Formerly printed in several volumes, it is now available in one volume.

Perhaps you can borrow these books from your husband's library. Or perhaps he can suggest other titles designed to meet the same need.

In addition to these three basic tools, do not overlook the cross-references in your Bible. These can be a great help in tracing all the related passages for a given subject.

Reading, the Basis of All Study

Correspondence courses are available through some Bible colleges for the advanced student. Take advantage of every help available. But remember that the best tool of all is the attention and time devoted to reading for comprehension.

The ability to become a self-feeder is directly tied to the way you read your Bible. For the self-feeder, the primary reading goal should be to read for understanding. Reading through the Scriptures in a year is a worthy goal. I have done this and expect to do it again. But the years I experienced the greatest growth were the years I wore out one section of the Bible as I read it repeatedly in order to understand it.

Try to grasp the highlights of what is being said. If that means reading an entire book to help you understand a specific section, do it. If that means reading the same section repeatedly, do it. Read with the attitude that the Bible is meant to be understood and the first level of understanding is to gain an overview of the passage.

Early in my experience, I began to read large portions of the Old Testament to gain an overview of events. A lifelong fascination with Moses developed as I repeatedly read about his life. One of my first discoveries was that Moses asked a lot of questions. In fact, he has been criticized for that habit in some commentaries. But as I studied the details of his life, I discovered a direct correlation between his habit and the growth of his faith.

The rewards of scriptural self-feeding are joy, spiritual strength and a stronger prayer life.

That discovery prompted me to move from the broad to the specific by doing a special study on the dialogues between Moses and the Lord. I examined every dialogue, looking for the details: What did Moses ask? How did God answer? How did Moses respond to God's answer? To date, this has been the most personally rewarding study I have ever done. No tools necessary—just a lot of reading.

Rewards of Self-Feeding

Joy
An unexplainable joy comes from discovering truths from the Scriptures for oneself, even when those same truths have been acknowledged by others, preached in fiery sermons and written about in books. The fact is that after much reading, after much concentration, you have seen a truth for yourself. And because you have seen it yourself, you will never forget it.

Spiritual Strength
Spiritual malnutrition leaves us vulnerable to the enemy. The condi-

tion is best avoided through a self-feeding program. A special strength comes from hard-earned personal knowledge of the Scriptures. This strength surpasses any strength gained by learning from others. This strength endures both the passing of time and the coming of trials.

A Stronger Prayer Life
The foundation laid through Bible study set the course for my prayer life. Although this could be illustrated in many ways, I will cite four specific areas.

1. Praying for the "irritants" in my life. We live in a fallen world. Life is full of unpleasant surprises, as well as downright meanness originating in the most unlikely places. In the Sermon on the Mount, Jesus reminds us that anyone can love someone who reciprocates that love. But we are called to love our enemies and pray for those who use us. I have learned to pray for those who make me angry. In the process, I have discovered that it is very difficult to stay angry at a person for whom I am praying. The person may not change, but I am never consumed by anger as long as I am praying for him or her.

2. Praying for straying loved ones. Each time I pray for one who strays, I take comfort in the fact that God loves the person more than I love him or her. Divine love far surpasses human love. To study the many passages that reveal God's dealing with His creation has given me a different perspective in praying for straying loved ones. I am moved to pray, and to leave the rest to God.

3. Praying for the world in which I live. The problems of our world are so overwhelming that we can become discouraged easily. Recently I have spent a major block of time in Psalm 119, which provides a pattern for praying for the world in which we live. The psalmist declares that it is time for the Lord to work because the world has made void His law (see v. 126). Anyone who watches the evening news can relate to such a prayer! Throughout the psalm, the writer prays for discernment of the Word and for help to keep his commitment to obedience. He positions his hope on (among other things) the fact that God is ultimately in charge and that although everything looks dark, He will one day right the wrongs and administer judgment and justice (see v. 119).

4. Praying for my personal ministry. From Moses, I learned to commit the work of my hands to God. I have always been acutely aware that all ministry should be done unto the Lord—whether public ministry or ministry behind the scenes or ministry in our homes. But only after I studied the life of Moses, and Psalm 90, which he

When we pray, we talk to God; but when we read His Word, He talks to us.

wrote near the end of his life, did I learn what it really means to commit our work to God. Moses was a man who knew great ups and downs, great victories and at least one great failure. He spent the last years of his life on a permanent detour. But he never stopped growing, serving and loving his God. At the edge of the land he was forbidden to enter, gazing at the Israelites who had paid scant attention to his pleadings, Moses prays, "Establish the work of our hands" (Ps. 90:17). It is like saying, "Lord it's all up to you, do with it what you would." This has become my pattern for prayer concerning the work of my own hands, wherever that ministry may take place.

In these four areas, and many more, I now understand better what I should pray for, and how I should pray as I have spent time in the Word. In college, we were often reminded that when we pray, we talk to God; but when we read His Word, He talks to us. As our "listening" skills improve, so do our "conversation" skills.

The Challenge Goes On

Each decade brings new and different challenges. Like many of my friends, I have struggled with issues such as establishing my identity, identifying areas of service that coincide with my spiritual gifts, building personal friendships and finding valuable "alone" time.

These are valid needs we must continue to address. But I have learned that the solutions include a built-in failure factor: friends can let us down; personal ministries fade away; support groups can dissolve; the combined family and church calendars can eat up all our "alone" time. But the woman who has become a woman of the Word will survive.

CHAPTER FIVE

idlife:
Crisis or Crossroad?

Sally Christon Conway

SALLY CHRISTON CONWAY EARNED AN M.S. DEGREE IN HUMAN DEVELOPMENT AND *family ecology from the University of Illinois in Urbana, Illinois. She is the cofounder and vice president of Christian Living Resources/Mid-Life Dimensions. Sally is a coinstructor at Talbot School of Theology and Denver Seminary, and adjunct instructor or lecturer at 14 universities, colleges and seminaries throughout the United States. She was a pastor's wife for more than 30 years.*

Sally is the author of two books, Your Husband's Mid-Life Crisis *and* Menopause, *the coauthor of seven books with her husband, Jim, and a contributing author to almost a dozen books. She has written articles for many Christian magazines and is the author, coauthor and contributor to five audiotapes. She has led conferences and retreats on marriage and family relationships in more than half a dozen countries, as well as appearing on many national and local TV and radio programs, and has received distinguished awards from four universities. The Conways have three daughters and seven grand-children. They live in Fullerton, California.*

⁓⁓⁓

I wanted to crawl under the bed. Or better yet, I just wanted to disappear. I did not want to run away or commit suicide; I simply wanted to cease existing.[1]

I felt so confused and frustrated, and my husband just lay there going off to sleep. I wanted him to talk to me. He was such a wise counselor for everyone else.

I finally gave a big sigh and crawled out of bed. In the dark, I walked into the living room. Strange emotions were boiling inside me. Most of all, I was wishing my husband, Jim, would wake up and be concerned enough to come and find me. I wanted to feel loved and comforted by him, but he did not seem to care about my raging turmoil.

Of course, I chided myself, *I should understand that he is very busy, pastoring a growing church. Tomorrow is a full day for him, with lots of meetings and appointments. I shouldn't expect him to take time for my troubles.*

In our previous churches, I had always shared in my husband's pastoring; now I felt left out and unneeded, like a discarded old box. The circumstances of my life were not actually much different from before; I was still active, involved and included, but I did not *feel* wanted or needed.

A wave of self-pity washed over me. Right after that, a wave of jealousy slammed into me. And before I could get myself stabilized, a third wave of plain old rejection would hit me. An old box—yes, I felt like a soggy cardboard box, bobbing just offshore. Soon I would be hopelessly saturated and sink.

Experiences like these were common to me during the last half of my 30s. My husband and I thought the problem was simply unique to me; some personal quirks I needed to work out. I struggled desperately, feeling immature and unspiritual. When I read the Bible, I seemed to find all the verses about my need to "die to self" and "crucify the flesh."

Then my husband and I began to meet other women who shared about their strange, restless feelings in the last half of their 30s or early 40s. Some were experiencing sexual feelings much as they had in early adolescence. One woman told me of being strongly attracted to the boys who carried her groceries from the store to her car. Others had gone as far as to have full-blown affairs.

We have all been shocked when women at this age have simply taken off, leaving husband and children. Some have run to the arms of another man, but many are just trying to "find themselves" and make the most of the years they have left. These are previously stable, loving and giving women. *Some of them are even pastor's wives.*

Why the Change?

My husband and I had already studied and written about men at midlife.[2] Now we wanted to know more about this chaos for midlife women, so we did formal research while getting our graduate degrees. We needed statistical proof that this was a real phenomenon and not simply a few isolated incidents.

Our results showed that as many as *75 percent of women do experience a moderate to severe midlife crisis* (inability to function normally in some areas of their lives). Their confused, desperate feelings and behaviors often have not been recognized as midlife crisis. Researchers have noticed, however, that high numbers of women at this age are returning to college or starting new careers. Early midlife is the most likely age for a woman to run away from her family.

But why? What has driven a woman to change so much? Many

changes are good and needed, but what does a woman need to know and do to make wise choices that won't ruin herself and other people?

Women in the last half of their 30s and early 40s are beginning their midlife years—whether or not they accept being that old. (Midlife is considered to be from ages 35 to 55.) The early midlife years are a transition time, going from young adulthood with energy, youthfulness and a long future, to being a midlife adult, which sounds as if one is about to go over the hill.

Midlife is a developmental stage, the same as childhood and adolescence are specific times of growth and change. Life evaluation is one of the key tasks during this time.

In a sense, a woman is at the top of the hill. Her early life is behind her, and the next half is ahead. Yes, the first part of life went too fast and the rest looks as if it is downhill. But going downhill is not totally bad. The roughest spot seems to be getting over the top.

Midlife is a developmental stage, the same as childhood and adolescence are specific times of growth and change. Life evaluation is one of the key tasks during this time. A woman is bombarded by questions: Who am I? What are my abilities? What are my experiences and interests? How shall I use my time? To whom—and how deeply—should I relate? What are my goals for the future? How important should God be in my life?

Beside this inner evaluation, a woman may be experiencing conflict between her dreams of how she thought life would be and the reality of what actually is happening. Her husband is not becoming more sensitive as she had hoped. Sometimes her children do very disappointing and frightening things. She still does not have enough money to decorate the house. She is not yet consistent in losing that extra weight or making other private improvements. Nothing is going as she had dreamed.

On top of her personal disappointments are cultural pressures. She is expected to look young, slim and alluring while she holds down a job, manages the household, cultivates a stimulating marriage, raises winsome children and keeps up with outside activities and friends.

By midlife, she is shocked to find that her body also is starting to let her down. She may find wrinkles and maybe some gray hair. She tires more easily and her skin won't hold still while she puts on eye makeup. She realizes she can't possibly keep up with society's image of youth and beauty.

A midlife woman also may have a low opinion of her worth and may not have a recognizable identity of her own. She has been preoccupied in assisting her husband's career success and ensuring her children's growth opportunities, but she has overlooked her own development. Because of these other important demands on her, she has neglected the most significant task God has given her: to nourish and develop herself, the unique and special gift from God.

In a Nutshell

A pastor's wife probably finds herself in an uncomfortable—and even ominous—position at midlife. But what can she do about it? She does not want the pressure to build until she blows apart and does rash things; neither does she want to shrivel and die.

In brief form, let's consider suggestions for help.

Be informed. The first is to be informed about midlife issues and what to do about them. She should read books and articles that not only give solid midlife information, but also support Christian values. Discussion groups and seminars can also help fill out her picture of midlife.

Evaluate life. She also needs to evaluate her life at this stage. Midlife has been thrust upon her without her conscious effort, but now she can take control by recognizing that evaluation is one of her tasks.

She is the one to come up with the best possible answers to her "philosophy of life" questions. She won't arrive at all the answers immediately, but she can meditate and deliberate over a period of time, asking the Holy Spirit to guide her thinking and resolutions.

Be realistic. This is a good time for a midlife pastor's wife to make some adjustments in her attitudes and actions. So reality does not match earlier expectations? She can alter what can and should be changed by her, and then accept and appreciate the rest. That includes her husband.

Culture's pressures. They don't need to rob her of the important things in life. God has His own set of norms, which just may include dressing attractively and knowing what is going on in the world. But His primary purpose is to make her into Christ's image—in her sensitivities, creativity, responses and other intangibles. Christ's image is far better than the world's image, or the image expected by the people in her ministry.

Changing body. The midlife body does change—and not usually for the better—but a woman can remember that her body's supreme purpose is to be the temple of the Holy Spirit. A midlife woman usually has been busy tending others and has neglected a healthy diet, exercise and rest for herself. If she is to have a usable temple, she needs to care for her physical needs. She also wants a beautiful temple, and will keep a balance between beautification efforts and service.

Personal identity and growth activities. The most help for me during my midlife confusion was the search for my personal identity and starting some growth activities. It was not that I had not been a busy person, but my busyness needed to be more in line with the personality and abilities God had given me.

Each woman's growth will take different forms. For me, it was to finish my undergraduate education and to develop and teach Christian education courses for adults. Previously, I had served whatever age group was without a teacher or any committee needing a worker.

Finding my individual identity did not mean that I gave up my roles of wife, mother, daughter and friend. I did not run off and start

Working through midlife concerns is a process, not a one-day miracle. Patience is a key word.

a new life. But understanding who I was—a Christian woman with a unique combination of abilities, limitations and interests—helped me to be a better wife, mother, daughter and friend.

Time and Tender Loving Care

Working through midlife concerns is a process, not a one-day miracle. Patience is a key word. A woman will come to healthy resolutions and attainable goals more quickly if she is encouraged by her husband and friends to vent her feelings, explore her musings and try new interests.

She can be honest with her Lord, pouring out her heart to Him. He already knows her questions and temptations and still loves her completely. She can be assured that He is producing a lasting work in her, although at times the sculpting and polishing hurt in some places.

We Are Not Finished Yet

All of life is filled with twists and turns, and women have the dubious privilege of a *second* potential crisis during their midyears:

MENOPAUSE!

Menopause generally occurs in the late 40s or early 50s, the average age being 51.5 years. In the strictest meaning, menopause occurs on the date of the last menstrual cycle of a woman's life. (Because a woman's cycle may be erratic, however, she does not know for certain that menopause has occurred until a year has passed.) The more commonly used meaning of menopause includes the months or years before and after the actual menopause. Women who undergo hysterectomies before menopause also have postmenopausal side effects.

Each woman may experience a wide variety of symptoms. One of the most universal is that she and her family think she is going crazy. She cries easily, gets angry quickly, is forgetful, is fearful and feels out of control. She also may have hot flashes, unusual aches and pains, sleeplessness, tingling and itching, heart palpitations, and other signs for years before and after the actual menopause occurs.

Her body is shutting down its estrogen production, which causes specific physical changes that also influence psychological functions. It is not all in her head. She is *not* making it up. Her body chemistry is causing her to be more jumpy, irritable and gloomy.

She needs to take concrete action to help herself, enlist her family in understanding her and get medical relief. Today's woman does not need to suffer all the consequences of menopause; help is available.[3]

For more than half of the 40 million menopausal women in the United States—and menopause is also a global event—the symptoms and difficulties disrupt their lives for several years. That is a lot of unsettled "woman-years" in the world!

No longer are women keeping menopause a secret. Yet, too many still try to endure without any outside help or encouragement. Well-meaning Christian women say that because menopause is God's plan, He surely would not intend for them to use hormone replacement or other help.

Just as God intends for us to use food to sustain our bodies, He provides other products and medical knowledge to help us, not only for menopause, but for childbirth, illnesses and injuries. When perhaps one-third of a woman's life is yet to be lived after menopause, it is good stewardship to keep that temple in shape. She should be as informed as possible and should enlist a doctor who will help.

Competent medical help will probably include hormone replacement therapy (HRT), which is restoring the supply of estrogen and progesterone the body makes naturally during the reproductive years. The good effects of keeping these hormones circulating in the body continue to be verified in the research labs and, most importantly, by menopausal women's personal experiences.

Hormone replacement protects against heart disease, osteoporosis (the silent bone thief) and emotional swings. In addition, a woman's skin and other tissues stay more supple. Dry tissues not only mean skin wrinkles, but also painful (and perhaps impossible) intercourse and the risk of more urinary infections.

When the question is raised about whether estrogen causes breast cancer, I consider what the best research shows: The chances of heart disease and osteoporosis are greater than the likelihood of breast cancer. If a woman does have an estrogen-dependent cancer, however, it may grow more quickly with estrogen replacement. But the cancer was in the body anyway.

The situation is similar to a charming, stray kitten we named Mittens. He started coming to our backyard to join our kitten, Mon Amie, at the feeding dish. As Mittens continued coming to eat, we noticed that he was growing. Our food helped him to thrive, but it did not cause him to be a kitten. He was already a kitten when he first found our yard.

Thus, estrogen does not cause cancer, but if a woman already has an estrogen-dependent cancer, estrogen can cause it to grow. The best medical research shows, however, that the benefits of estrogen far outweigh the potential hazards.

Hope for Our Future

Menopause may be a particularly difficult time for many pastors' wives, given the peculiarities of their profession. But—rough or easy—the menopausal years can become the years in which great personal growth takes place, priorities are refined and a refreshing peace rules in the midst of a still-tumultuous life.

Another part of God's plan is that the pastor's wife will make the transition into a long, productive era of life still to be lived for His glory and for the benefit of her husband, children and grandchildren.

> In old age [she] will still produce fruit and be vital and green. This honors the Lord, and exhibits his faithful care (Ps. 92:14,15, *TLB*).

Notes

1. Jim and Sally Conway, *Women in Mid-Life Crisis* (Wheaton, IL: Tyndale House Publishers, 1983). Expanded details can be found in this book.
2. See Jim Conway, *Men in Mid-Life Crisis* (Elgin, IL: David C. Cook Publishing Co. 1978), with reprints until the present; and Sally Conway, *Your Husband's Mid-Life Crisis* (Elgin, IL: David C. Cook Publishing Co., 1980), with continuing reprints.
3. Sally Christon Conway, *Menopause: Help and Hope for This Passage* (Grand Rapids, MI: Zondervan Publishing House, 1990).

urviving the Stress Factor

Anna Hayford

ANNA HAYFORD AND HER HUSBAND, JACK, HAVE MINISTERED AT THE CHURCH On The Way in Van Nuys, California, for 25 years. Two years after they were married, Anna and Jack both graduated from LIFE Bible College in Los Angeles, California, with honors. After graduation, Anna assisted Jack in beginning a church in Fort Wayne, Indiana; they then served as national youth directors for the International Church of the Foursquare Gospel in Los Angeles; she assisted him in his tenure as dean of students at LIFE Bible College as well as when he served as president of their alma mater. Anna's genuineness and unaffected wholesomeness are an example for all women. In the midst of a busy world and a continually mushrooming and demanding ministry, Anna is supportive, keeps her joy, her sense of humor and her peace. The Hayfords have four children and eight grandchildren. They live in Granada Hills, California.

❦

Stress!

It screams at us from the covers of women's magazines every month. And who understands more about stress than pastors' wives?

Our lives are filled with juggling everything from women's groups, social events, church services to cooking, laundry and marketing. No other profession requires the wife to be such a vital part of her husband's career as the pastorate.

Stress shows itself in a variety of ways: the phone is insistent, the counseling never ends, questions are always being asked, the constant demand to be involved in everything that happens inside or outside the church, the baby showers, weddings, funerals, parties, graduations and so on. How do we keep our sanity in such a setting?

Criticism

One element that contributes to stress for a pastor's wife is criticism. I have found that criticism of me is much easier to handle than criticism of my husband or one of our children. I know my husband to have such a pure and tender heart that when people speak against him I find it hard to be objective.

I remember when we first came to our current pastorate (The Church On The Way) and the church started to grow rapidly. People would come to me after every service either offering suggestions of how we could change something or have some criticism. They always wanted me to get an answer from Jack for them or persuade him to change whatever they wanted changed. On their behalf, I would faithfully ask Jack about all these things until I realized the time we had together was being taken up by their questions or suggestions. We came to the point of argument over some of these things because they were actually robbing us of our "together" time.

I decided I needed to say something to those who criticized, something that would break this cycle. After a time, I suggested to them that they write a letter to Jack, or in the case of criticism of him, I

The Lord built a wall of protection around me, and I am happy to live within that wall.

would just say, "Well, you know your pastor." These things seemed to satisfy them and it was not long before they realized I was not going to be their messenger girl and the cycle eventually stopped.

Criticism of me has not been too difficult to handle. I have always believed that the Lord built a wall of protection around me, and I am happy to live within that wall. He has also blessed me with the gift of naïveté. I say blessed with naïveté, because at times people would say things to me and another person would question their intent, but I seemed to always see the good in what they had said.

One time when I answered the phone the woman on the other end of the line said, "I just called to tell you I really love you." That much would have been great, but she went on. "I couldn't say that three weeks ago because then I didn't think you were that neat a person." Instead of feeling negative about what she said, my first thought was, *I'm glad she is growing in the Lord.* This woman was fairly new to spiritual things. After sharing the incident with one of my confidantes, her comment was, "What did you ever do to her?" Such a thought had never entered my mind, and for that I was grateful.

Before Jack and I accepted the position at The Church On The Way in Van Nuys, California, I kept asking the Lord what my part of the pastorate was to be. I know the Lord impressed on me that I was to just love the people. I felt comfortable with that and have tried to live with that objective. This year (1994) will mark 25 years at The Church On The Way. I must say that I have done many other things, but loving the people has remained my priority.

Burnout

The stress experienced by many pastors' wives contributes to burnout. When I reach the end of my rope, I know myself well enough to know I have to spend some time alone. When I say to my dear Jack that I need to be alone, he always says, "Except for me?" I have never had the heart to say, "Right" or "No, not with you either." (Of course, NOW he will know.) I must be entirely alone.

During those alone times, I do whatever I feel like doing. It may be just sitting down without the stereo, TV or radio on; nothing—just complete quiet. I don't have to go away from home, but I do need to be alone in the house. I let the answering machine answer the phone and I do what I want to do. Sometimes I read, do needlework or work in the yard, but only if that is what I really want to do. It is also nice to sit in a hot tub and let the water wash away the tenseness in my muscles. Another thing that is very restful to me is to fill the bird feeders in our backyard and just watch the birds. Watching the birds eat, feed their young and dart here and there makes me feel better because I am not the one who is up and busy.

Sometimes changing my surroundings helps me. Last January, after all the holiday celebrations were over, I went to spend a week with one of our daughters. Both she and her husband were at work every day so I was at their house alone—only their dog, Sam, to keep me company during the day. He is an old dog so he didn't want to do any more than I did!

Outside Help

When Jack and I first entered the ministry, we had very little money. We never lived near either of our parents so we did not have the help of family when we needed someone to lean on in times of burnout. The Lord was gracious to us in providing older couples who were like parents to this inexperienced young couple who had just graduated from college.

I will never forget Walter and Ilse Werk, who were an answer to our prayers when we pioneered a small church in Fort Wayne, Indiana. They supported us in so many ways during those early years. They were just there. They encouraged us, prayed for and with us, had us to their house for wonderful German meals; and that at a time when we had a low food budget.

Brother and Sister Risser also provided encouragement to us. They pastored a church a little more than a hundred miles from us, but at times when we were discouraged we would drive to their house. They were always there with open arms to greet us and love us back to emotional health. What a blessing to have older ministers who care for the younger ones. Now we have the privilege of being on the giving end.

Time Management

Sometimes we contribute to our own stress. Time management has always been a challenge to me. Jack is spontaneous, so it has been impossible to follow the suggestions on those dish towels that tell you what to do every day of the week. Monday you wash clothes, Tuesday you iron, and so on every day of the week.

I was raised in the Midwest, outside the city, and our life was well ordered. We had to do chores in the morning, attend school, do afternoon chores, eat supper, do our homework and then go to bed. In the summer, we had to tend the garden and do the canning. So our life was simple and well planned for us all the time.

Then I met and married a man who was a part of everything, and I never knew when he would be home for dinner or who he would bring home with him or how many. It has certainly made my life interesting—never a dull moment. It was hard for me to be flexible, however, and not know what was going to happen on a given day. When our children were little, we would often go on a picnic in half-an-hour notice. Everything was put aside, a lunch was fixed and we always had a wonderful and happy time. It is important to learn flexibility, especially when you are making memories with your family.

Accept Only the Lord's Assignments

Over the years I have learned to manage my time, and one of the best ways is to accept only the assignments the Lord assigns you. Many times, as pastors' wives, we want to fill every vacancy in the church and neglect our first priority—our family. I know many pastors' wives who have no choice other than to fill some of those vacancies. In the beginning of our own ministry, we did everything. We cleaned the church, took turns playing the piano, taught the two Sunday School classes, performed the special music, did the preaching, took care of the building, did the home calling and so on.

Make Lists

Making lists helps to keep me focused on the things that must be done. By making a list of tasks, you can arrange the chores by priority. Organizing your errands is helpful and is a time-saver. It is rewarding when you can mark things off your list.

Have Children Help

My salvation in keeping house came in the help of our children. They started doing small things at an early age and as they grew they assumed more responsibilities. I was absolutely lost when they were no longer available, especially when it came time to entertain; and we entertain a lot.

I taught the children to do their chores thoroughly and helped them by organizing the supplies. I always put their bedding in bundles; so when they went to the linen closet to get sheets to make their beds they picked up one bundle that included a fitted sheet, a flat sheet and a pillowcase. This helped both them and me by keeping the linen closet neat.

Cleanliness...But Do Not Be Driven
I like to accomplish everything I have scheduled to do every day, but sometimes that isn't possible. Don't let yourself be discouraged by those things that didn't get done today. Most things can wait until tomorrow. Also, do not be driven by being overly "clean." Please don't take that statement as a cop-out for not cleaning your house. One pastor's wife said that if she woke up in the middle of the night and noticed a cobweb on the ceiling light she would get up and clean it right then. That is what I mean by not being "driven."

I was advised by a seasoned minister's wife to have the dishes washed and the beds made. Having those two things in order helps the house to look clean.

Early to Bed for Children
One of the things I did that was helpful to me was getting our children to bed at an early hour. It is surprising how much you can accomplish in the evening when you don't have little ones to watch and care for. Bedtime was 7:00 P.M., which gave me some time for catching up on chores, getting a little rest for myself or spending some time with my husband. Without some long, quiet evenings, I don't know how I could have made it through the days with three little ones. We had three children under the age of five—number four was born when our third child was seven years old.

A Place to Grow

In spite of stress, burnout and the difficulty of time management, being a pastor's wife is an exciting and fulfilling life. In the midst of the challenges, we are always required to grow in many different ways; ways that are far beyond us at times.

When our church became a congregation of 2,000 people, I was overwhelmed by the size; my mind would not comprehend it. I felt guilty and frustrated because I could no longer greet everyone by name. As a child, my home church consisted of 150 to 200 people and I knew everyone's name. No wonder embracing a church of 2,000 was such a task for me.

Many times I said to the Lord, "How could you take a little

The Lord is able to sustain us and make us adequate where He places us to serve.

Nebraska girl, put her in the middle of a big city, in a church that is growing by leaps and bounds, and expect her to keep her sanity?" I would pray and pray about the situation, and was finally impressed by the Lord to make a trip back to Nebraska by myself. After discussion with Jack, we arranged for someone to watch our four children. I packed my bags and flew home to Nebraska. While there I would go to my room at night, read the Word, pray and always end the prayer with that same question—Why?

One night as I started to ask the question, it seemed as if the Lord put a large cork in my mouth and said, "Don't ask that question again. You are no longer a little Nebraska girl." I knew by impression that He was challenging me to think bigger than I had ever thought. It was as if He were saying, "This is only the beginning."

I knew the Lord did not mean for me to make a disclaimer of being from Nebraska. I just knew I was out of line in what I was asking and how I was feeling, and it took a startling encounter for me to be able to hear what the Lord was going to say to me next.

After asking forgiveness for my insensitivity to the Lord's call and actually sort of murmuring, I told the Lord I was ready to move on and to listen to His voice. At that point, the Lord spoke to me forcefully. He said, "You don't need to know everyone's name. I know their names. All I told you to do was to love them and I will give you all the abilities you need to accomplish everything else I call you to do."

I was free! Free to love! Free from guilt! Free from facing a problem that was too large for me. When I returned home to California, life became much easier. I found that people of the congregation didn't even expect me to know all their names. I have been expressing my love to these dear people ever since, and in return I feel greatly loved by them.

I pray for each pastor's wife who reads this chapter. I pray that you will have an encounter with the Lord that will free you; whether you need to be freed from stress, burnout, criticism or some other problem that is too big for you to overcome on your own.

The Lord is able to sustain us and make us adequate where He places us to serve.

CHAPTER SEVEN

*W*hen Home Is Havoc, Not Haven

Pamela Hoover Heim

*PAMELA HOOVER HEIM EARNED HER M.A. DEGREE IN COUNSELING FROM DENVER
Seminary, Denver, Colorado. She is the national director of women's
ministries for the Baptist General Conference, is a retreat and seminar
speaker and teacher for women's groups, a lecturer and consultant on
women's ministries and has a limited psychotherapy practice. She is
the author of five books, including* Nurturing Intimacy with God *and*
The Woman God Can Use. *She has also been a magazine editor, is the
author of a daily devotional commentary on the whole Bible and*

wrote a curriculum package for Compassion International that included a movie. She has been involved in ministries with Young Life and Campus Crusade for Christ. Pamela was a pastor's wife for four years. She and her husband, Lowell, have two grown children and two grandchildren. The Heims live in Colorado Springs, Colorado.

Beth's* husband engaged in homosexual affairs, but she did not expose him because she believed God expected her to guard his ministry.

Allie's husband punitively gave her and their children the silent treatment for weeks at a time. Domineering and contemptuous, he kept them in line through fear.

Sondra felt obligated to submit to the debasing sexual activity depicted in her husband's pornographic magazines. She hoped she would satisfy his warped desires so that he would remain "faithful" and not destroy his ministry.

When Judy was thin, her husband accused her of having affairs; when she put on weight, he called her ugly.

These women have two things in common: they are ministry wives and victims of their husbands' abuse.

Abuse in Pastors' Homes

Although we would like to think otherwise, abuse happens in pastors' homes. Almost any Christian counselor can confirm this, yet silence—as seen by the lack of research on the subject—perpetuates the myth that a Christian minister would not abuse.[1] The tragedy of such abuse is its double abuse of power: that of a spouse or parent and that of a church leader.

*Names have been changed. Also, I have primarily related second-person accounts rather than stories shared with me directly because: (1) I do not want any pastor's wife whom I have counseled or will counsel to fear violation of confidentiality; and (2) my second-person sources are impeccable and congruent with my own observations.

Abuse may be psychological, emotional, physical and/or sexual. Psychological abuse is controlling another by fear, including threats of leaving, rejecting, exposing a "secret" or inflicting harm. Emotional abuse damages the soul through harsh criticism, demeaning and shaming remarks, derogatory name-calling and other verbal assaults. Most people understand physical abuse as shoving, shaking, hair pulling, slapping, kicking, punching and beating. Not all physical abuse leaves marks on the body.

A factor in abuse is that hurt people hurt people. Abuse victims tend to abuse if they have not adequately resolved their own painful issues.

A wide range of behaviors constitute sexual abuse. For a wife it may be rape, being psychologically coerced into intercourse or hurt during sexual activity. Children are abused by any sexual touching, showing them pornography, inappropriately intruding and inquiring into their sexual behavior, "teasing" about their sexual development, sexually derogatory name-calling (bitch, whore, slut) or treating them as a surrogate spouse.[2] One study indicates that fathers from conservative churches who have a strong religious taboo against incest still commit incest.[3]

A Need to Control

How could a *minister* sit on his wife and spit in her face while speaking in tongues, as one woman reported? The reasons for abuse are perhaps as many as there are abusers. Because the common denominator in all abuse is power and a need to control or dominate, it is not surprising that abusers often hold an authoritarian, patriarchal view of marriage and family.

Emotionally Wounded Male
Another factor in abuse, as Christian psychologist, Sandra Wilson, says, is that hurt people hurt people. Abuse victims tend to abuse if they have not adequately resolved their own painful issues. Becoming a Christian does not necessarily cure emotional wounds any more than it guarantees physical healing.

Whatever the reasons, *nothing excuses abuse*. And no matter how blessed a pastor's ministry may appear, God never condones his abusing. Abuse is always wrong and always the responsibility of the abuser regardless of where *he* places blame. He *alone* is accountable for his choices and actions.

Wives' Tolerance of Abuse

Denial
Why do wives tolerate abuse of themselves or their children? Well, many deny it, "It's not really abuse." Or they minimize it, "He just gets upset at times." If a wife grew up in an abusive home, abusive relationships may feel "normal." Often a wife feels embarrassed, guilty and at fault because she judges herself defective, and her husband's blame feeds this. Some wives see abuse as God's punishment for their sins, such as having had premarital sex.

Threats
Some women live with abuse because of threats, "I'll kill you, divorce you, tell people you're crazy." Another fear is losing the marriage; some wives put up with abuse because they genuinely love their husbands and desire to keep the marriage together no matter how bad it is. Also, if a pastor's wife exposes her husband's abuse, he may lose his job and livelihood and thus she loses financial support and her parsonage home—economic dependency may keep wives quiet.

Submission

One reason some women tolerate abuse is their belief that God expects them to submit to their husbands even to the point of injury and death to themselves or their children. Often an abusive husband

Abuse has a profoundly harmful effect on the abuser and the abused. Children, because they link minister-father with the heavenly Father, may later rebel to the point of rejecting God.

misuses the Bible to build a case for his indefensible behavior. But if a man who does not provide materially for his family "has denied the faith and is worse than an unbeliever" (1 Tim. 5:8), how much more evil is the man who damages their bodies and souls?

Harmful Effects of Abuse

Children

Abuse has a profoundly harmful effect on the abuser and the abused. Children, personally abused and abused by seeing Mom abused, carry deep wounds. Because they link minister-father with the heavenly Father, they may later rebel to the point of rejecting God. They are more susceptible to addictive behaviors to numb their emotional pain. They may repeat abusive family patterns themselves; sons following Dad's model are especially liable to devalue and demean women and children.

Wives

Abused wives endanger their lives and those of their children because abuse often escalates. They teach their children, especially their daughters, to take abuse passively, that might makes right, and implicitly that God condones out-of-control rage and violence. Other results of abuse manifest in physical problems, depression, anxiety and overeating, to name a few.

Men

Men are rarely motivated to deal with or repent of their violent anger if they are not confronted with the evil of their abusiveness. "If that person's irresponsible behavior is covered up...that makes it easier for him...to continue the destructive pattern."[4] A wife who "interrupts the law of sowing and reaping in another's life" disrupts one of God's best means of teaching her husband.[5] Ignoring abuse rewards and reinforces it.

Steps in Dealing with Abuse

What can you do if abuse makes your home more like hell than heaven?

The first step is to *name abuse and call it sin.* I have seen healing happen after a woman understands and admits that her husband's scaring her and the kids by yelling and throwing things is abusive.

Second, *tell yourself the truth.* Face it, the abuse has not been (and probably won't be) prayed away—perhaps you are asking God to do what He wants you to do for yourself. The abuse also won't stop even if your husband often acts contrite, cries, apologizes, promises you it will never happen again and buys flowers for you after an abusive episode. He needs help to set limits on his behavior.

Third, *get clear on God's value of women and His plan for wives in marriage.* Read the books suggested at the end of this chapter.[6] Talk to a Christian family-life teacher.

Fourth, *seek professional counseling or a support group for abused women*. You need objective input because abused women lose perspective on what is and what is not appropriate behavior. You need somebody to encourage you when you are tempted to settle for abuse, because it seems easier to do nothing. They will coach you in how to speak the truth in love: "This behavior is your choice, you're responsible, you've hurt me and this family, you've used the Bible as a club to control us." Counselors will help you set healthy boundaries: "You may not treat us this way anymore, you must get help, take responsibility or we'll do what's necessary to stop your abuse of us. I'm prepared to act on Matthew 18:15-17."

A counselor or support group will help you know how to take steps to protect yourself from possible violence resulting from confronting abuse. *Never antagonize your husband if you think he may hurt you or your children, unless you have an action plan for getting away to a safe place.*

Frankly, some abusers do not want to change, admit wrongdoing or get help. If through prayer you come to believe that separation is the only way to protect your children and yourself from abuse and to force your husband to realize the seriousness of his problem, remember that his abuse, not you, caused the separation. You are doing this *for* him, not *to* him, hoping that this consequence will pierce his hard heart.

Finally, always cling to God's great and precious promises (see 2 Pet. 1:4). You are God's cherished child; His plans for you are good and loving; He strengthens you and He is your gentle husband.

Recommended Reading

Relevant to Difficult Marriages:
Alsdurf, James and Phyllis Alsdurf. *Battered into Submission.*
    Downers Grove, IL: InterVarsity Press, 1989.
Dobson, James C. *Love Must Be Tough.* Dallas, TX: WORD Inc., 1983.
Cloud, Henry and John Townsend. *Boundaries.* Grand Rapids,
    MI: Zondervan Publishing Company, 1992.
Johnson, David and Jeff VanVonderen. *The Subtle Power of Spiri-*

tual Abuse. Minneapolis, MN: Bethany House Publishers, 1991.

Langberg, Diane. *Counsel for Pastors' Wives.* Grand Rapids, MI: Zondervan Publishing Company, 1988.

Leman, Kevin. *The Pleasers: Women Who Can't Say No and the Men Who Control Them.* New York: Dell Publishing, 1987.

Strom, Kay Marshall. *In the Name of Submission.* Portland, OR: Multnomah Press, 1986.

On Childhood Sexual Abuse:

Allender, Dan. *The Wounded Heart.* Colorado Springs, CO: Nav-Press, 1990.

Peters, David B. *A Betrayal of Innocence.* Dallas, TX: WORD Inc., 1986.

Notes

1. In the 1989 National Association of Evangelicals survey of pastors' wives, 24 reported spouse abuse. This number is probably low because many equate abuse only with bruises and broken bones. Nationally, the average of wife abuse is 14 percent.
2. See Dan Allender's book (Recommended Reading section) for an excellent definition of sexual abuse and its results.
3. Vincent E. Gil, "In Thy Father's House: Self-report Findings of Sexually Abused Daughters from Conservative Christian Homes," *Journal of Psychology and Theology* (La Mirada, CA: Biola University) 16:2, pp. 144-152.
4. Diane Langberg, *Counsel for Pastors' Wives* (Grand Rapids, MI: Zondervan Publishing House, 1988), p.96.
5. Henry Cloud and John Townsend, *Boundaries* (Grand Rapids, MI: Zondervan Publishing House, 1992), p. 41.
6. See the Alsdurfs' book (Recommended Reading section) for an in-depth discussion of the biblical perspective on marriage, submission and abuse.

iscipling:
Catch the Vision

Anne Ortlund

ANNE ORTLUND AND HER HUSBAND, RAYMOND, MINISTER TOGETHER IN RENEWAL *Ministries at conferences all over the world. She was a minister's wife for 31 years. Anne graduated from the University of Redlands in California with a major in organ, and also won the Associate Degree of the American Guild of Organists. She was the organist for Charles E. Fuller's "The Old Fashioned Revival Hour" radio broadcast for 15 years.*

Anne has had many compositions published, among them "Macedonia," the first place award-winning theme hymn of the World Con-

gress on Evangelism held in Berlin in 1966. Anne is the author of more than a dozen books, including Up with Worship *and* My Sacrifice, His Fire: Weekday Readings for Christian Women. *Her book* Children Are Wet Cement *received the Christy Award as the best marriage-family book of 1982. The Ortlunds have 4 children and 11 grandchildren. They live in Newport Beach, California.*

What an exciting new beginning it is, whenever a pastor and his wife catch a vision for discipling members of their congregation! Let me tell you how this concept has grabbed my heart, and my husband, Ray's, as well.

It's always been God's method for His workers to strategize to reproduce themselves, and to build strength into those who will later replace them in spiritual leadership. Let me give you an Old Testament illustration of this, and I'm praying God will make your heart alive with application for your own ministry—and your husband's.

Elijah and Elisha: Discipling in Scripture

When Elijah had gone through major depression after ministering all by himself (see 1 Kings 19), God comforted him with a disciple—Elisha. I have to believe that Elisha was the cream of the crop of younger men. (Always look for the "cream" of the younger ones to disciple!)

In those days, placing your cloak over the shoulders of another signified succession or replacement (see 1 Kings 19:19-21). It was a little like Jesus saying, "Follow Me, and I will make you fishers of men" (Matt. 4:19). Or in other words, "Come do what I'm doing; join Me to learn, and then replace Me."

Elijah didn't *explain* his throwing his cloak; he just did it. But Elisha understood exactly what he meant, and he ran after Elijah (who had already taken off down the road). "Let me kiss my father and mother good-by," Elisha said (1 Kings 19:20, *NIV*).

Now, retreating Elijah said a strange thing: "Go back!...What have I done to you?" (v. 20, *NIV*).

This was no emotional entreaty—Elijah trying like everything to persuade somebody to be his disciple—and that's an important cue for you and me. He seemed to be seeking to be "loose": "I'm not trying to dominate you. This is your decision." I have tried to "hang loose," too, in asking young women to be in my groups—although the prayer behind the scenes has often been intense!

But when the disciple is more excited than the discipler, that's ideal! Elisha went home and got rid of everything (see v. 21). He literally "burned his bridges behind him." As Jesus said, "If anyone desires to come after Me, [be discipled] let him...take up his cross, and follow Me" (Matt. 16:24). I would much rather have three disciples wanting to "go for broke" with God—than six who have to be "pulled along."

And so for 10 happy years Elijah discipled Elisha, as together they taught and encouraged young seminarians.

Near the end, Elijah tested Elisha's "staying power," seeming to try to shake him off (see 2 Kings 2:2); but Elisha hung on.

"So the two of them walked on" (2 Kings 2:6, *NIV*). Beautiful! It's so important, so precious, when discipler and disciple are committed to walk for a period of time together. So far, 150 younger Christians have walked with me—usually for a period of a year—occasionally one at a time, but more often in groups of four to six. It is so wonderful to "walk on" together—for Jesus' sake!

Then, just before the end of Elijah's life, Elisha begged for a double portion of his spirit (see 2 Kings 2:9). He wasn't saying "I want twice what you have," or "I want to be twice what you are"—not at all. Both knew that the double portion was the inheritance of the Jewish firstborn. He was saying, "Elijah, I want to be considered your most special son, and you, my dear father."

And Elisha's prayer was answered. This is why, when Elijah was caught up in the whirlwind to heaven, Elisha cried, "My father! My father!" (v. 12, *NIV*). Be greedy for God's great blessings in your life, and teach others to be greedy! Go hard after God—together!

And guess what? God answered Elisha's prayer literally: Twice as many miracles are recorded performed by Elisha as by Elijah! I am so thrilled that practically all my past disciples are still walking strongly

To relieve *leadership, you make committees and boards; but to* reproduce *leadership, you make disciples.*

with the Lord, but I am most thrilled of all that several have become far more strategic and effective disciplers than I am.

Make Disciples, Not Committees

Now, this is what many pastors and wives need to come to see: to *relieve* leadership, you make committees and boards; but to *reproduce* leadership, you make disciples. Committees provide only for the present need, but disciples build for the future.

Committees and boards are indeed good and necessary. In Exodus 18, Moses delegated much of his judging work to a committee of other spiritual leaders. In Acts 6, the apostles delegated food distribution to a board of godly deacons. In each case, the relief was wonderful. But neither group, as a group, is ever mentioned again: When the members died, the group died.

Committees do not have babies. They are sterile, they are non-producing, they are "eunuch" servants. But disciples contain the seeds of reproduction, life and multiplication.

I disciple a small group of gals each September to June, with the understanding that in the succeeding years they will turn around and each disciple a few others, who will in turn each disciple a few others and so on.

Recently, a few of my former disciples surprised me with a luncheon to which they invited all my former disciples, plus all their disciples, plus all their disciples and so on. It took a lot of research to find them all. From what they were able to uncover, from my weekly discipling around our dining table of five or six gals each year, 600 invitations were sent out! The multiplication rate is incredible.

This is how you build a strong church from the inside out. Your growth does not come from onlookers being attracted to a superstar in the pulpit until a more scintillating star arrives at a church down the street. You start discipling an intimate few of your eager ones,

Discipling will build strength and godly continuity into a church.

who will each do the same the next year. And without your hardly knowing what has happened, you will soon have dozens of "pastors" in your church; they'll be pastoring each other.

Discipling Builds Continuity

Is this really true, that discipling will build strength and godly continuity into a church? Ray and I have seen it wonderfully happen.

Look at Moses. He discipled young Joshua, and when Moses died, Israel's spiritual health went right on without missing a beat (see Deut. 34:5,9).

But what was Joshua thinking of? He was never recorded to have discipled anybody; he only formed committees (see Josh. 18:3,4). So when Joshua died, an era ended (see Judg. 2:7,8,10), and the Israelites disintegrated fast into idolatry (see v. 11 ff.).

Since the very beginning, in each of Ray's four pastorates—totaling 31 years—I have tried to function so that the church would be stronger, not weaker, when we moved on. I've never held offices; I just coached behind the scenes to help women function where needed. My thought was to not leave "holes" when we were through. In a sense, that was discipling, though in the early years I didn't know enough to identify it in that way.

But at Lake Avenue Congregational Church in Pasadena, California, Ray and I began discipling in earnest, by design—which is described in his little book *Lord, Make My Life a Miracle*[1] and for more specific "how to's," in my book *Discipling One Another.*[2]

Ray began discipling guys and I, gals; and from time to time we would together disciple a mixed group of marrieds and singles. The results were life-changing for the two of us, and church-changing as well. God began a slow-burn revival in our flock that lasted for years.[3]

And when we left? Hey, in the year and a half between pastors the church grew. And they also built a million-and-a-half-dollar education building. You'd think they could have been thoughtful of us enough to suffer at least a little bit when we left, but they didn't!

Pastors' wives sometimes ask me, "Isn't discipling playing favorites?" Hopefully, your husband will be teaching and modeling discipling as well as you, so that your people will begin to understand that this is biblical and right. And then, if you'll be careful to disciple your groups for only a year or so, they'll get the picture that if they aren't in the current group, they might be in one later on.

You see, out of many disciples, Jesus deliberately picked 12 (see Mark 3:13,14), and out of the 12, particularly 3. And we never read that the other 9 disciples minded! Why did He do it? Jesus was looking ahead to the book of Acts; He was preparing leadership for the days when He would physically no longer be around.

Here is a wonderful discipling verse for you; it's Jesus' own words, spoken to His Father in John 17:19 *(TLB)*. As you read it, may your heart become an altar of obedience to God, to give yourself away to others:

> I consecrate myself to meet their need for growth in truth and holiness.

Notes

1. Ray Ortlund, *Lord Make My Life a Miracle* (Ventura, CA: Regal Books, 1974).
2. Anne Ortlund, *Discipling One Another* (Dallas, TX: WORD Inc., 1979).
3. For more particulars on how this works out in your own life and in the life of the congregation, see Ray Ortlund's *Three Priorities for a Strong Local Church* (Dallas, TX: WORD Inc, 1988).

CHAPTER NINE

*M*entoring:
Woman to Woman

Gail MacDonald

GAIL MACDONALD IS A GRADUATE OF THE UNIVERSITY OF DENVER, AND HAS BEEN a pastor's wife since 1972. She has spent much of her time meeting with marketplace women in and out of their church community. She is a speaker at seminars, conferences and churches across North America, as well as in other countries. Gail is trained to administer and interpret the Myers-Briggs Temperament Indicator and consults churches and other nonprofit organizations regarding placement and conflicts in relationships. She has written three books, including

High Call, High Privilege *and* Till the Heart Be Touched *(coauthored with her husband, Gordon).*

After having lived in the heart of New York City for 4 years, where Gordon was the pastor of Trinity Baptist Church, the MacDonalds returned to Grace Chapel in Lexington, Massachusetts, in March 1993, where they had previously served for 12 years. The MacDonalds have two children and two grandchildren and live in Lexington, Massachusetts.

∽✦∾

I love nurturing. And I love trying to convince women that one of the greatest challenges open to those of us over the age of 45 is to sink ourselves into the lives of the young. It alarms me that many of us are choosing to put our energies into the marketplace rather than helping young women move toward spiritual maturity.

For years, I thought all of my mentors were dead people I read about in books. Along with biblical characters, they became my friends. Amy Carmichael taught me how to rejoice in suffering. Mary Slessor showed me how to be content and enthusiastic in spite of the circumstances. Catherine Booth demonstrated the importance of writing letters of depth and insight to those who are closest to me. Sarah Edwards proved the value of maintaining my walk with Christ at all cost. On and on goes the list of mentors from books.

In recent years, however, I have realized that I am marked by a host of mentoring contemporaries. For instance, I think of my friend, author and speaker, Margaret Jensen, whose zest for life, travel, faith and humor, in spite of experiencing loss and cancer, has challenged me. Or my own mother who has taught me over and over the graces of giving, forgiving and holding loosely to things. Or my aunt Georgia, who was single all the years I knew her but had once been married and had a child. But when both husband and child died tragically, she determined to devote herself to teaching handicapped children as well as being involved in the lives of her nieces and nephews. This she did for the next 35 years! Although she did not know it, she was mentoring me.

One day my husband, Gordon, and I realized that the majority of our own mentors are single people. Did they take more time to grow deep roots in Christ because their loyalties were not divided by marriage? I am not sure, but the fact remains. Although Gordon had many mentors who were proactive in their interest in his growth, I

All of us need three kinds of people around us: (1) elders who walk in front of us; (2) peers who walk beside us; and (3) the young with whom we walk.

did not. Perhaps that is one of the reasons I am so concerned about it. All of us need three kinds of people around us: (1) elders who walk in front of us; (2) peers who walk beside us; and (3) the young with whom we walk.

I have no doubt in my mind that the younger people eagerly await our active involvement. Two years ago a gifted teacher at Grace Chapel, Linda Anderson, had just such a burden and began a program she calls Mom to Mom. Older mothers take younger mothers under their wings for a year. In small groups, they discuss the biblical principles they were taught from a lecture Linda gives each week. Today, the demand is greater than space and mentors allow, and Mom to Mom enjoys a long waiting list. Groups across the country are writing and asking for the material because they also sense the need.[1]

Why We Avoid Mentoring

Some have called mentoring the Titus 2 principle. Paul mandated to Titus that older women should teach the younger women. But, we often hesitate. Why are we afraid of mentoring?

One reason could simply be that our culture esteems individualism. Is it not valued to "do it my way" rather than seek counsel from others? Don't we hold up as models those who seem strong without another's input?

Several years ago when Gordon and I went through a dark period in our lives, I was startled at how few women in my life had anything of value to say to me. I came to realize that they had never experienced my being in need of them. I had been their leader, the "together one." Little wonder they did not know what to do with me when I needed them.

In the same way, if the young women do not seek wisdom and insight from the more mature women, the older women won't feel needed and will find other interests to fill their time. It is instructive to remember that Jesus leaned on His friends, although He knew they would fail to be adequate helpers. "Pray with Me," Jesus says (see Matt. 26:40); let Me lean on you. Are we greater than our Master?

Second, we tend to isolate our elders rather than remind them of their wealth of wisdom. Years of experience and insight go to waste when our older women enter retirement communities away from the younger women. What would happen if we could convince them that they had things to teach us that we badly need?

About 11 years ago when I was developing a team of leaders for a Bible study at Grace Chapel, I decided to ask two women who were in their upper years to join us. They were dumbfounded and found it hard to believe they could be effective. I asked them to trust my instincts and give it a try for a few months. At the end of that time, we would reevaluate whether it was wise for them to continue. Both of these women went on for years as effective facilitators, and I am still getting a yearly letter from one of these women about her present enjoyment in this ministry. The bottom line? Many of the older generation will have to be convinced they have something to offer the young.

Third, could it be that we fear the generational gap? After all, we view things in such different ways. Yet, is it not possible for us to appreciate the differences and accept them, so that we will be invited to influence the next generation?

What the Young Need from Us

After four years, we have just said our good-byes to our congregation in New York City. As a parting gift, they gave us a beautiful scrap-book of letters and pictures. Because most of the congregation are in their 20s and 30s, we felt like mentors to many of them. It was inter-esting for us to read what was most important to them as they reflect-ed on our years together.

Being close enough to *observe* us in real life was a key point. The big city made that far more natural than suburbia, because we spent so much time together on public transportation. Scripture was being lived out in us when we were not even aware of it: praying for peo-ple on the spot, caring about those who drove our bus or tram, being hospitable to other passengers. Of course, having the young people into our apartment created a wonderful setting for learning and affir-mation to take place. Many of them had never seen a couple serve as a team in their own home.

The young people also *took courage from our life experiences,* which presupposes our being vulnerable. They probably learned more from how we handled our failures and weaknesses than our successes. If we are transparent, then they will find the courage to also look within themselves and be open about their weaknesses. I asked a group one day, "What do you need most from older believ-ers?" Several of them said, "Help us heal our wounds." If that is where they are beginning in the process of becoming like Christ, then we have to be aware of how we have been healed of our own wounds and be open about the process.

In *A Step Farther and Higher* (Multnomah Books, 1993), I have written about my own journey in "wound healing" and how I had to own up to being an "elder brother" and "doubting Thomas" during a time of discontinuity in my faith. Relearning how to trust God was a new thing for me, as I had always believed easily. But my difficult experience has been a helpful bridge to many of the young. In men-toring, we are hoping to ensure spiritual maturity, but for some we have to begin with the open sores that hinder growth.

Finally, the congregation *sensed our unbounded confidence in them.* We have found that many of the young need to be loved unconditionally and to have someone believe in what the life of Christ can do in them. Most of my mentoring relationships have involved learning how to be partners in a shared task. Such opportunities might include ministry to the homeless, remedial reading,

Jesus did not take volunteers as disciples. He put His finger on each one; surely not because they were already leaders, but because He saw potential in them.

Habitat for Humanity, caregiving or helping others study the Scriptures. The latter two have been where I have invested the greatest number of years.

Ten Necessary Traits for a Mentor

For instance, before inviting women to become a part of a team of facilitators who would help other women mature through Bible study, I was looking for certain attributes, often embryonic, before I approached them. Being able to say that I had observed these traits in them was my way of beginning to show my unbounded confidence. And I could affirm that this confidence would only grow as we worked more closely together.

It is noteworthy that Jesus did not take volunteers as disciples. He put His finger on each one; surely not because they were already leaders, but because He saw potential in them. People value our taking the time to note their strengths and they respond eagerly to our initiation.

Here is my list of 10 necessary traits for a mentor:

1. Has devotion to Christ and building His kingdom;
2. Is dependable;
3. Is sensitive to others;
4. Keeps short accounts in relationships;
5. Lives as steward, not owner of things or people;
6. Has suffered or failed and used it to benefit growth;
7. Is generous with honest affirmation;
8. Shows mouth control;
9. Has active prayer life;
10. Has listening teachability.

After nine years of leading my team, and using these 10 traits as my grid, I had to intervene only once in a relational conflict between two leaders. The rest of them worked out any conflicts in constructive ways, while we maintained an amazing oneness.

How It Is Done

The mechanics of mentoring can be read about in many books. I appreciate *Disciplemakers' Handbook* by Alice Fryling (InterVarsity, 1989). Make your methods fit your personality, ever asking the question, How have others encouraged my growth? Obviously, the material you use needs to fit the task. If your goal is to meet each week one-on-one, your material and concerns would be far different from what I have suggested. Remember, most of what women learn from you will be picked up through observing your attitudes and reactions to everyday life. Christ fleshed out in us—what a hope! The rewards are immense. Ask me.

Note
1. For more information about the Mom to Mom program, write to Linda Anderson, Grace Chapel, 3 Militia Drive, Lexington, MA 02173.

CHAPTER TEN

Proposal for Preparation

Mary Lou Whitlock

MARY LOU WHITLOCK GRADUATED FROM BELHAVEN COLLEGE IN JACKSON, MIS-
sissippi. She was a pastor's wife for 10 years. Mary Lou served as Chris-
tian education director for a church in Jackson, Florida, for six years.
She leads, along with other wives, the work of Mrs. in Ministry, the
seminary program for wives of seminarians. This program is now
completing its fifth year. She is a conference and retreat speaker and
speaks at regional women's meetings of her denomination. Her hus-
band, Luder, is president of Reformed Theological Seminary, and they

divide their time between the two seminary campuses in Jackson, Mississippi and Orlando, Florida. The Whitlocks have three children and three grandchildren.

❧

High hopes, hard realities, incredible joy, ultimate responsibility, deep satisfaction, great pain, lasting fulfillment. Could anyone have a more fascinating job description? Ministry is a job that takes you from the highest highs to the lowest lows of discouragement and disappointment. Called of God to serve Him. The highest privilege on this earth.

The previous chapters show the huge expanse of the work of ministry. Upon reflection, few would want to enter such a field without some basic training. But what can you do to get ready for such a calling? How would you prepare to go into the fields "white for harvest" (John 4:35) as the wife of a man called to teach and preach the gospel of the King of kings and the Lord of lords?

NAE Survey Results

In 1989, approximately 600 ministers' wives responded to a survey, conducted by the National Association of Evangelicals, about their ministries, their lives, their needs and a wish list for help (see appendix 1). The responses were often inspiring (the personal fulfillment expressed by those seeing changed lives), convicting (a lot of hard work is going on in the ministry), discouraging (where are the encouragers for those frustrated or struggling in leadership?) and in some cases, heartrending (deep wounds and depressing pain exist in the ministry). Many wives pleaded for help with ministry skills (counseling, discipling, teaching, etc.) and wished they had been the recipients of more help and advance preparation before they were launched into varying degrees of leadership roles. Short of enrolling in seminary herself, where is such help available for a woman who, with her husband, desires to serve the Lord?

Seminary Training for Pastors' Wives

I am among those who believe that the seminary setting is the most natural and positive place a wife can prepare herself with confidence, personally and professionally, for ministry with her husband.

The seminary setting is the most natural and positive place a wife can prepare herself with confidence, personally and professionally, for ministry with her husband.

Denominations and seminaries, however, have been slow to recognize the need for holistic training of couples and even slower to carefully examine data that shows the devastation of ministries, as well as marriages, when the spouse cannot or does not adjust to ministry demands and needs.

According to some denominational studies, half of all couples who leave the ministry prematurely leave because of the wife's unhappiness. Seminarians themselves often do not understand how vital training is for their spouse and for the effectiveness of their ministry together. Wives must be willing to set aside the time for training. Congregations and denominations must press those they send to seminary to seek classes and programs for wives, and seminaries must put these needs high on their priority list.

If a program were available to help women in seminaries, what would it be like? How do you decide what a helpmate needs to know to keep her life balanced, her spirits lifted and to enable her to participate meaningfully in ministry? Reformed Theological Seminary has attempted to establish a program, offering a three-year-rolling curriculum for wives that meets once each week, and tries to cover major areas of ministry. I have been privileged to work with some faculty wives of the seminary who have a passion for the work of the church and the assistance we might give to prospective ministry workers. This program is called Mrs. in Ministry. Instituting such a program is not easy. It is possible, however, especially if the seminary looks at the total view of the couples' ministry. My own experience during my husband's seminary training helped me to know that even a limited program was of benefit in ministry work.

Personal Experience

During our years in seminary, we had a group of student wives who met once a month with faculty wives. We came with eager anticipation, usually to hear one of the seminary professors teach us in his area of discipline. This was a great treat and a learning experience, providing a taste of what our husbands were experiencing in the classroom. Occasionally, a pastor's wife came to tell us what things were really like in the church and to answer the multitude of questions we asked.

An evening with a pastor's wife only raised the level of anticipation for another meeting so we could move to new questions that popped up into our minds. We earnestly wanted to do well and to fit into what was expected of a pastor's wife. None of our group, as I remember, had been raised in the manse or parsonage with role models, so we were hungry to get inside the brain of someone who lived "in the glass house."

About the only existing book relating to the life of the pastorate in those days was Carolyn Phillips Blackwood's book, *The Pastor's Wife* (now out of print). We read it and digested it chapter by chapter. We worked at learning and sharing ideas that would help us in our future work, but our program efforts were scattered at best. No one had a "big picture" vision.

The advantage we did have was that almost all of us had been raised in the church. We had a model of what kind of roles or influence might typify a pastor's wife. Most of us had fine models in our experience. Today, far fewer prospective pastors' wives have that background. Many become Christians in adulthood and have never been a part of any church in their childhood or young adult life. They have no reservoir of models to imitate or to encourage them. They are just beginning to establish a framework of ideas regarding their future responsibilities for ministry and how they can best apply them. Many women today actually have a greater need for biblical and practical programs than we did. Many women today must also learn to balance ministry and family needs as well as a vocation outside the home.

The seminary experience then becomes very crucial at this point. Watching and participating with other faculty wives in sporadic attempts to produce programs for student wives over the years convinced me that a more long-range program having definite goals was imperative. A structured program of planned helps is critically important. Scattered attempts to hit subjects of importance just won't get the job done. We tried, as many schools do, and still we were not alleviating the senior-wife panic that was occurring more often than we wished as husbands approached the great day of graduation and their call to the first post.

Some wives were almost paralyzed with fear about their future—partly because they did not know what to expect, partly because they felt unprepared and also because they feared failure. Very few of us fare well in situations where we are unknowledgeable, unprepared and frightened. How can the church expect a vibrant, joyful and happy ministry when the pastor who leads them is barely able to persuade his wife to hold things together? The demands of the church, her husband, her children plus perhaps a job, those expectations she places on herself can exhaust and frustrate her. She sees few ways to cope and even less possibility of things getting better. Help needs to come before this scenario takes form.

Wives in Training

Titus 2 gives an injunction for older women to teach younger women in the ways of faithful Christian living. How wonderful to have fellow

Christians who have already been in ministry (the pastorate, missions, counseling, music, youth work, evangelism, etc.), teaching and helping those who are beginning the journey. A well-thought-out curriculum led by those who love the Lord and His work can be of inestimable value in getting new workers off to a positive, strong beginning. This is crucial, I believe, for solid ministries.

One denominational official who visited Reformed Theological Seminary said that in his travels across the United States, he had never seen a growing healthy church that did not have a committed wife and open home at the core of the work. That is a sobering but also wonderful thought. A great home, a committed marriage, a nurturing situation for family, church and friends. What could be more needed and satisfying when it is present or more awful when it is not? Healthy relationships undergird a couple for life. Our aim should not be less than that.

We need to tell seminary wives of the joy of ministry and the benefits to self and family that God gives so freely to those who work for Him. Of course the work is constant and hard. What in life is not hard that is truly worthwhile? But God blesses the family, the couple and the congregation of the leaders who give themselves to show the love of God. Even in the darkest and most discouraging times, we see the hand of God working His will. Sometimes it is impossible to see how God will bring anything substantial out of a situation, but Scripture assures us that He will, and our experience in life verifies that truth. Faith, trust, patience and endurance are marks of the Christian that sustain us through hard times. These truths need to be taught, talked and lived for the wife in training.

Teach Right Attitudes

It is not unusual to hear the negatives about life in ministry. There are, sadly, many hurtful stories of those who have tried to minister and suffered greatly at the hands of those they sought to serve. But these commentaries cannot and should not be all that our student wives hear. What about the fulfillment of seeing changed lives and knowing you were privileged to participate in these sometimes radical turnabouts?

What about the joy of working side by side with others who share a like faith? What about the family nurture and enrichment possible for the ministry worker's family from those believers around them?

Along with other faculty wives, I have loved teaching and working to give positive and cheerful encouragement to seminary wives regarding ministry. And I can honestly do that because our two pastorates were some of the happiest years of our lives. We loved the church. Our children loved the church, and actually our biggest adjustment was leaving the church to come to the seminary faculty. Some people still tell funny stories about our adjustment—or lack of it.

Our youngest daughter was just six years old when we left our beloved congregation in East Tennessee. When asked why we moved to Mississippi, she replied in great sorrowful tones, "God told my daddy to come here, but I never heard Him!" She continued by telling her listeners that her brother and sister did not like it either and her mother did not come! (I had stayed behind to coordinate packing and moving while my husband, Luder, went ahead to get the children started in school.) So much for a great start in our new vocation! It serves to illustrate, however, how much children can love growing up in a church family and how painful it is to be separated from such love and nurturing.

Teaching these attitudes about ministry, as well as skills and helps, over a period of time and in a steady and consistent way can build a sense of desire to serve and a deeper understanding of the privilege of service. And, it is challenging. Ephesians 6:12 says that we fight against principalities and powers—real satanic forces. We must arm ourselves with truth and wisdom to do God's work in a fallen world. Are we willing to discipline ourselves and to sacrifice whatever is necessary to do this?

Wouldn't it be interesting to use the U.S. Army's commercial: "Be all that you can be" and add "in the Lord's work"? A little paraphrase of Philippians 4:13! Seminary training for women should be an encouragement to run the race with joy and enthusiasm, using the time we have wisely. We should face the hard realities of ministry: the long hours, the sometimes unappreciated and unheeded work we do in the name of Christ, the countless meals served sometimes to angels unaware—as the Scripture says (see Heb. 13:2)—and the zillion other tasks and duties that fall into the category of ministry. Learning that we will have to cope with cantankerous souls and complaining communicants will take the edge off when the reality of ministry sets in. Every vocation has problem people—the church is no different. Our attitude, however, will make all the difference in the world in how we approach the difficulties.

Learn Spiritual Discipline

I cannot imagine any kind of ministry training that does not begin with personal spiritual development. Learning to deepen daily communion with the Lord and to become more obedient in daily lifestyle begins a true path of spiritual discipline. Learning how to pray, praying and developing a pattern of inner spiritual enrichment is a primary goal. Obviously, many walk this path in a profound way before they ever come to seminary, but others walk it in a less disciplined way. Growing deeper in our walk with Christ comes with age, maturity and commitment to spend time in significant ways to be in the presence of God.

First-year seminarians study the devotional life of the saints for the purpose of developing their own pattern of spiritual growth. Should we, may we, do less for wives of seminarians? Does not their "skill" in knowing how to have a deepening spiritual walk become foundational to their marriage, ministry and life commitment? So it is here that training must begin. John C. Ryle has said in *Holiness*, "[We] have neglected the sober realities of daily practical godliness. There has been of late years a lower standard of personal holiness among believers than there used to be."[1] We cannot expect the Church to exhibit more godliness than its leaders.

Basic Training

Romans 12:1 calls us as believers to be living sacrifices. And learning to discipline ourselves for spiritual service is the next step. Attempting to master skills in communication in marriage, parenting and other relationships is vital. Some basic counseling skills, including crisis counseling, is critical. Who in ministry does not face death and dying, unplanned pregnancies, potential suicides, cancer and a myriad of other diseases and problems? Skills in presenting the gospel, teaching, giving a testimony, leading a devotional or Bible study, introducing speakers, conflict management, time management, entertaining in creative and inexpensive ways, working with children, youth and parents, music, missions, being a witness in the nursing home or in the home of a child with a crippling disease are all areas to be conscious of and to consider. No one is called to do all of these things, but knowing elements of the work and understanding how to approach them takes anxiety and fear to a much lower level.

Studying spiritual gifts and knowing giftedness is enabling. How can we serve Christ effectively if we are unsure how to serve best? Confidence comes with understanding ourselves and our gifts, then being willing to use those gifts. We are far less afraid to step through doors of opportunity when we are confident about our strength and realistic about our weaknesses. Obviously, no course or magic number of training years can ever cover every situation we will face, but training should provide a foundation from which most situations can be addressed.

Help for the Reluctant Wife

Can the seminary help the woman who reluctantly arrives on campus with her husband after having spent many years in secular work? She never dreamed she would be drawn into "professional" ministry. She is not sure why she is on a seminary campus or what her role might or could be. She does not see herself as a spiritual teacher or leader of any sort. She may want out. Is there help for her? The faculty wives or other designated leaders, as well as the curriculum programming, should be a great encouragement to her. This can happen in various ways.

First, all women are encouraged to see themselves as belonging to Christ who paid a great price for their salvation. As a recipient of such wonderful and undeserved grace, do we not want to serve our Lord with our life in the best way we can? That does not require a woman to become a great Bible teacher or speaker—but it could. It is quite satisfactory to be a growing Christian who is caring and sen-

I would say to any seminary wife—push yourself to the limit to find the pearls you will need for life's ministry. No sacrifice is too great to learn what you need to know.

sitive, who supports her husband and seeks to be a friend to those who need her. Few people on earth could not do that. Being a supportive wife, a loving mother and providing a setting where the lifestyle of faith can go on is, according to Proverbs 31, the highest of honors. Would anyone who claims the name of Christ not be willing to at least try these tasks?

Often, when presented with these possibilities, I have heard both young and older women say, "Oh, I can do that. I want to do that, but I thought you had to be a teacher or gourmet cook or soloist, etc." Certainly those gifts *are* valuable in the Kingdom, but a woman does not have to play the piano or teach to be an effective and memorable servant in the kingdom of God. Our job is to emphasize this fact and to encourage consistent Christian living in the home and in the world. The ministry does not consist of clones, and women need to know they honor God best as they serve Him by using the gifts and personality He has given them.

It is imperative to remember and teach that God uses the people who willingly seek to be obedient to Him. Recall that Sarah thought she was too old; Esther felt unequipped and without proper position; Moses felt unable, Isaiah, unworthy; and we feel many of the same inadequacies just as acutely. However, in 2 Corinthians 12:10, Paul acknowledged that when he was weak, he was strong—because of God's grace. God can and does use the life submitted to Him. We must trust Christ who promised, "I will be with you."

Seminary: No Piece of Cake

I am for publicizing the fact that seminary is no piece of cake. Training is hard, demanding and sometimes downright unpleasant as it stretches us. But it is needful in various ways for both spouses. I would say to any seminary wife—push yourself to the limit to find the pearls you will need for life's ministry. No sacrifice is too great to learn what you need to know. Do not pass up an opportunity to learn, to grow, to stretch. Every time you do, you forfeit knowledge and growth in skills that might be useful.

Should you expect to do great things for God if you are unwilling to sacrifice yourself to be properly trained to serve? Admittedly, the many ministry areas to become familiar with, knowledge to acquire and the list of practical helps that are needful are long; but is anything too much when we want to do our best for the Lord? Let's set our goals during the student years to learn what it takes for the long haul while the opportunity presents itself.

Let's push our seminaries and denominations to provide help for all who will give their time, energy and emotions to learn. And then let's press on to work for the Lord while there is yet time.

Note
1. John Charles Ryle, *Holiness* (Phillipsburg, NJ: Evangelical Press, 1979).

etirement:
A Word Not in God's Dictionary

Kathryn Stephens Grant

KATHRYN STEPHENS GRANT HAS BEEN A PASTOR'S WIFE ALL HER MARRIED LIFE and is currently cochair with Evelyn Christenson of the Women's Track of AD 2000 North America. She graduated from Coker College (South Dakota) and received the alumni of the year award in 1993. She and her husband, Worth Collins, served as missionaries in Japan for 20 years. After returning to the United States, they pastored at Temple Baptist Church in Washington, D.C., where Kathryn became executive director of the Department of Baptist Women in the D.C.

Baptist Convention. She also joined Charles Colson's Prison Fellowship International as founding vice president. In that capacity, she spent two years as representative at the United Nations in New York, as well as traveling internationally for the organization.

During Kathryn's time in Washington, she was chosen as mother of the year for Washington, D.C., and she wrote the book Making the Most of the Best of Your Life *(1990). After retirement, the Grants moved to West Palm Beach, Florida, but have spent six months in each of the past two years in Tokyo, Japan, for a special mission assignment with their foreign mission board. The Grants have four daughters and five grandchildren.*

Reflections

She tiptoed across the uncarpeted empty room, pausing momentarily. Her discerning eye pierced into the corners of the room, surveying every inch of the wall and floor. The committee from the church would find the parsonage immaculate. One remaining chair in the kitchen became a haven for a few minutes of thought.

Future pastors' families will reap the rewards of our recommendation to allow the pastor to purchase his own home. Educating our children took priority over our plans for future housing, yet, in our Father's provision, we do have a small house waiting.

There will be no private study for my husband like the ones the churches have provided. But we can add shelves to one of the bedrooms. How he's looking forward to having time to read the books he has collected all these years. In the past, there was never enough time. The people of the church took first place in his pastor-heart.

I wonder how long this freedom will last before the pages of our calendar are again full, pushing us on to the next day, the next activity. Together we must consider carefully how to structure our schedule, lest the relentless clock devour our time with meaningless motion.

The years have romped along, dizzying in their rapidity. This will be the first time in our married life that I will not be a pastor's wife, and my husband will not be the pastor of my church! We must learn how to be

members in a new church. I am determined to be a friend and encour-
ager to my pastor's wife, just as many dear friends were for me.

Now we must leave a generous, loving church. Pleadings from
many in the church family tempted us to live nearby, but we would
never put such an obstacle in the way of the next pastor and his wife
who are called here to minister.

The reflections of this retiring pastor's wife mirrors the thoughts
of many wives of retiring pastors. At age 65 or 70, the pastor and his
wife face the prospects, the process, the transition and finally, the
reality of retirement. Some couples prepare with cheerful optimism;
others will simply be forced by time to cope. True, scores of women
in various fields of work also retire, and others having home careers
share retirement with their husbands, but for the pastor and his wife,
additional adjustments are involved.

For those who have dedicated their lives to special Christian service,
who have walked as best they knew in the will and guidance of our
Father, retirement should be neither a time of sadness nor a time of fear.

The imperative is to discover how the experience, the new
lifestyle, can be an example of authentic Christian living. Indeed, such
a passage becomes a challenge and opportunity for demonstrating
God's faithfulness "to never leave us or forsake us" (see Heb. 13:5),
and for affirming that through His strength we can do all things.

Retirement becomes a remarkable way to demonstrate all we
have taught and often quoted from the Scriptures. Our loving Father
is sufficient in His grace and love to provide for our every need—
material and emotional. On such a strong foundation of faith and
having joyous anticipation, we can confidently entrust our future to
His love and care.

Distorted Depictions of Retirement

The usual depictions of retirement rarely illustrate the true lifestyle
that is ahead. One such picture often presented is that of a just-
retired couple boarding a huge, expensive motor home, driving off

into a future of perpetual travel. Another is of a vibrant young couple who live on a green golf course overlooking a sparkling lake encircled with palm trees. Equally unrealistic for the vast majority of those retiring with the best years of ministry ahead is that of invalids whose days are spent in wheelchairs, having every waking hour consumed by constant visits to the doctor.

A Biblical Example: Joshua

How utterly different is our heavenly Father's perspective on this passage of life. A fascinating glimpse of His viewpoint is found in Joshua 13:1.

One day God engaged Joshua in conversation. Joshua knew from experience that when God spoke to him, he would receive a work assignment. Perhaps he had been wondering when the last assignment would come. God made it clear that resting was not in His thinking. One can almost hear God chuckle as He speaks. If the slightest thought of retirement had entered Joshua's thinking, it was dispelled when God said, "You are old, advanced in years, and there remains very much land yet to be possessed" (Josh. 13:1). God then proceeded to give the 85-year-old Joshua the most exacting, difficult task to date, one lasting for 25 more years.

Throughout the Bible, allusions to retirement are not given as a reason for a Christian man or woman to think, "I've done my part, now it's time for me to rest and let someone else do it."

Rather, Scripture reflects in every passage that God has a continuing objective for our lives. Many successful retirees find such rich opportunities for ministry in His kingdom that they wonder how they ever had time for a job previously.

Opportunities to Serve

In this day, both massive needs and creative opportunities abound. Every talent can be matched with a need. Latent talents can be brushed off in a course at the local community college or a summer at an elder hostel.

Considering the training and experience a pastor and his wife have, opportunities to serve are expanded to include overseas needs for teachers, pastors of English language congregations and volun-

Knowing God's will is as significant for the mature seeker as it is for the young seeker.

teers to assist missionaries in various projects. Vast lists are available that offer meaningful volunteer service in the church, community organizations, hospitals, prisons and rest homes. Volunteers work with children, teenagers or the very elderly. (See Resources for Ministry in *Making the Most of the Best of Your Life*, Hannibal Books, 1990, by this author.)

God has an exclusive place and need for each of His children. The last year before retirement can be a time to prayerfully seek His guidance. Knowing God's will is as significant for the mature seeker as it is for the young seeker.

Retirement: The Crown of Life

In Genesis 28:15 *(KJV)*, God says, "Behold, I am with thee...for I will not leave thee, until I have done that which I have spoken to thee of." Because the pastor and his wife have a deep knowledge of the Scriptures they have studied for many years, because they are familiar with intimate assurances in prayer, because they have walked with God through varied life experiences, their ministry in retirement years may well be the crown of a life of Christian service.

To some retirees, God may present the highest calling of all—to be a dedicated *pray-er*. Such a calling demands strong self-control; a strict time set aside in a daily schedule so that closet time becomes the day's priority. By having a well-kept prayer journal, a request list may be gleaned from the needs of missionaries, churches, friends and neighbors. In an astonishing way, this quiet ministry seems to bring a myriad of people and needs right to a couple's own doorstep.

Dollars and Sense

All reflections on retirement, however, are not of joyous anticipation. Were we to put God's searchlight into our minds, lurking in a dark corner are fears that rob us of confidence in the future.

To really profess the honesty we desire, let's get down to dollars and *sense*. No pastor's family has known affluence. The security of a church's monthly paycheck is not the same as the government's social security check. Years of depositing in the denomination's retirement plan now makes logical sense; although contributions to retirement plans often seemed impossible when dollars were few and far between for a young, growing family.

Pastors and wives who planned early by balancing their need for a retirement plan with the family needs in earlier years are more likely to approach a different budget and lifestyle without being debilitated with fear. When change comes, the couples who have years of experience walking hand-in-hand with our heavenly Father are most fortunate. Should uncertainty or fear dare invade their minds? Those who have the grace of years to draw upon have a far different perspective. They can look back to the lean times, spiritually or materially, and recall the amazing way God provided for their every need.

They have come thus far knowing God's faithfulness across the years, whether in college, in seminary or the pastorate. The Lord was faithful when babies came, when the car broke down, when as seminary students we traveled miles to a church and had barely enough money for gas and received a jar of beans as an honorarium.

Be assured, "Grace [often in the most unexpected way] hath brought [us] safe thus far, and grace will lead [us] home."[1] God's multiple, exciting promises are constant and fresh. They are also gener-

Conventional wisdom looks at the height of romance as the time of youth and the honeymoon of the just-married. The world just has not learned a deep, dark secret many retirees know but have not been telling!

ous. Look, as He so beautifully clothes the lilies of the field. So will He care for His own. They are His representatives and through them He will display His truth and His faithfulness. Finances can be their secret and His. He who sees in secret always takes note of His children's needs and He will show forth the abundance of His resources.

Husband and Wife Relationship

And how does retirement affect relationships, especially the most precious of all, the husband and wife relationship? If those preparing for retirement could really see the future, they would know that someone has made a big mistake. Conventional wisdom looks at the height of romance as the time of youth and the honeymoon of the just-married. The world just has not learned a deep, dark secret many retirees know but have not been telling!

This time together after retirement often becomes a renewal for love and sharing. For a marriage that has lasted through the bumps of a pastor's ministry, time has brought a mellowing and acceptance of each other that overrides and overlooks each one's foibles. Husbands and wives become more exciting lovers and best friends. The new breath of freedom from imposed schedules grants time to linger over a morning cup of coffee, time to laugh together over shared experiences. Still, they have learned to give each other space to pursue individual choices and schedules. Retirees need not be thought of as Siamese twins.

Closely budgeted money does not rule out shopping for a bottle of faint perfume or for dressing attractively for each other. Equal sharing of home duties opens time to play together, whether on the proverbial golf course or to explore and wander here and there, even feasting on a bowl of Chinese noodles.

Relationship with Children and Grandchildren

In the experiences of many, retirement provides a magnificent occasion for cementing and bonding with adult children and the magical grandchildren. Young parents today need every encouragement and support.

The love-trust relationship between grandparents and grandchildren is a special gift planned by our heavenly Father. Into their tender uncritical hearts, we can instill our love of Jesus and share in their nurturing and spiritual growth.

Difficulty in the parent/adult-child relationship may arise if their parental role is criticized, if visits are too often or too long, or if out of self-pity or boredom too much demand is made for the adult child's time and attention.

Wise retirees will set limits, without guilt, on the amount of free child care that fits into their schedule. Neither will they allow themselves to be depended on to rescue adult children from constant financial incompetence. From such prayerful planning, adult children will become most treasured friends.

Finishing the Race with Joy

Let us return to our retiring pastor's wife where we left her sitting in the uncomfortable kitchen chair. Her Bible is open on her lap and she reads with greater understanding a favorite passage relating Paul's experience as he prepared to leave Ephesus.

> You know,...what manner I always lived among you, serving the Lord with all humility, with many tears...kept back nothing that was helpful,...I go...not knowing the things that will happen to me there, except that the Holy Spirit testifies....But none of these things move me; nor do I count my life dear to myself, so that I may finish my race with joy, and the ministry which I received from the Lord Jesus, to testify to the gospel of the grace of God....I have coveted no one's silver or gold....And remember the words of the Lord Jesus,..."It is more blessed to give than to receive."...he knelt down and prayed with them all (Acts 20:18-24,33-36).

The doorbell rings, but our retiring pastor's wife does not move. With her pencil she underlines the phrase, "that I may finish my race with joy." The doorbell rings again. She glances up briefly but looks down again at the words she has just underlined. Smiling, she takes the pencil and adds a final mark—a big bold exclamation point!

Note
1.   John Newton (1725-1807), *Amazing Grace*. Public domain.

CHAPTER TWELVE

ommitment:
The Key to Contentment

Carol Rhoads

CAROL RHOADS IS A GRADUATE OF WHEATON COLLEGE IN WHEATON, ILLINOIS, and pursued graduate studies at Pasadena College, Pasadena, California. She is a former school teacher and past chairman of the Upper Merion Christian Women's Club in Philadelphia, Pennsylvania. She is chairwoman of their church's women's outreach program and prayer ministry, as well as the women's conference sponsored by the church. Carol is an accomplished pianist, is active in follow-up visitation of church visitors and members and does counseling; she also coordi-

nates and cohosts semiannual Holy Land trips. Carol and her husband, Ross, have three children and eight grandchildren. They minister at Calvary Church in Charlotte, North Carolina.

❧✦❧

It happened without warning. It was the kind of phone call a pastor and his wife dread. My husband, Ross, and I were in Jerusalem leading a group of church friends through the land where Jesus walked. We had spent the day on the Mount of Olives, recalling how Jesus had wept over Jerusalem, and how He would return some day to that very place. We had stood at Calvary, and had read the Scriptures that told of His sacrifice for our sins. We had wept openly at the empty tomb and had sung with great joy, "Up from the grave He arose" and "I serve a risen Savior."

Then the disturbing news came like a shock of cold water poured over our heads. One of our dearest friends had left a note after more than 30 years of marriage: It was over, he was gone, please call his wife, she does not know yet.

We could not believe it. As a pastor's wife, you know the problems that are typical in any congregation. But these friends were both proactive and deeply involved in the life of the church. We never thought they would have this marital problem.

What went wrong? How could he? Why didn't we sense something was wrong? We thought we knew them. Had we failed? Why did we miss it? Why would he throw away his marriage? She is so beautiful, so lovely, so caring, the mother of his children and a grandmother of several children. Where had the love gone? What was he thinking? Didn't he care about her feelings and all she had done for him? Where were all the promises? What happened to his commitment?

Commitment Produces Strength

Commitment—that's it. Our friend had broken his commitment. He had chosen to walk away from a lifelong commitment, and the promise "till death do us part." It was no longer to be "as long as we both shall live," but "as long as we both shall love."

Commitment is fast becoming a thing of the past; something that God demands, our parents practiced and we know to be right, but now it is, "Everyone [does] what [is] right in his own eyes" (Judg. 21:25).

To whom and to what should I be committed? It is not enough that my husband has given his life to serve the Lord and His Church. It is imperative that I do the same thing—out of love for my Lord and His work. Riding on my husband's commitment, without personally yielding to Christ unreservedly, is a sure path to failure and disappointment. Commitment to God's work must be preceded by devoting myself to the Lord Jesus, His plans and purposes.

As a teenager, I had promised the Lord that I would serve Him in full-time Christian work. Because I loved and taught the Spanish language, I assumed this would mean missionary service abroad.

The turning point came at Wheaton College. After dating a popular basketball player for two years and occasionally talking about marriage, I became increasingly agitated with "our" plans. He had not committed himself to full-time work and I had. Repeatedly, I tried to convince him that he could fulfill his calling on the mission field. We argued constantly. In the space of the next two months, I was a passenger in three automobile accidents. God was definitely getting my attention. I refocused on God's calling, and my dating with the basketball player terminated. (The very next night my future husband dated me for the first time.) My submission to God's will and my obedience to His leading brought me heightened direction, great relief and marvelous peace. That deliberate commitment to please God was to be followed by many more commitments in the next 38 years.

"Even Christ did not please Himself" (Rom. 15:3), but submitted Himself to His Father. "He humbled Himself and became obedient to...the death of the cross" (Phil. 2:8). Jesus renounced His own will, His plans and desires in order to please His Father. As His child, and as a pastor's wife, the object of my love is my heavenly Father. The expression of that love will be demonstrated by my obedience. To be committed, to give myself to God, requires a clear understanding of God's purpose for me on a daily basis.

God's purposes are expressed in His commands. Jesus said, "If you keep My commandments, you will abide in My love, just as I have kept My Father's commandments and abide in His love" (John 15:10). The greatest commandment is to "love the Lord your God with all your heart, with all your soul, with all your mind, and with all your strength" (Mark 12:30).

God is worthy of our love and the only One deserving of our life's commitment. Selfish ambitions and personal desires are to be put aside in the light of God's love and sacrifice for us, demonstrated in the giving of His Son. Being self-centered is an antithesis to loving God; complacence must be replaced by commitment, self-interest gives way to self-denial. We belong to Him. He expects our love and allegiance. He demands it. He will accept no less than total submission of our hearts and wills. Then we will experience that increased love for God, which will result in pleasing Him.

If we are not committed, submitting ourselves daily to God's purposes in loving obedience, we will soon find ourselves overburdened, overworked, overstressed and without strength. To depend upon God in daily commitment is to seek His face and to receive His strength. "My help comes from the Lord" (Ps. 121:2). Frustration comes when we fail to do this. Then we experience lack of joy instead of love and compassion for others. Then worry, discouragement and a critical tongue are more evident than peace and contentment in God. In Psalm 105:4 the Psalmist exhorts: "Seek the Lord and His strength; seek His face evermore."

Jesus speaks in a reassuring way in John 15:4,5: "Abide in Me, and I in you. As the branch cannot bear fruit of itself,...I am the vine, you are the branches." The believer cannot produce fruit without the life-giver: Jesus Himself.

Then comes that beautiful promise to every believer. If you and I yield ourselves to the Lord, He works in us through the Holy Spirit, and our committed lives will "bear much fruit." Jesus said, "For without Me you can do nothing" (John 15:5).

Dependence on God

Some years ago my husband and I were in Austria, visiting in a small rural hotel. The phone service was not as efficient as it is in the United States, and we tried to place a call to one of our sons at home. After repeated dialing, we called the owner of the hotel to help us, explaining our inability to reach our destination. He sensed our frustration and emphatically exclaimed, "I must dial for you. You cannot get through by yourself. You must understand, without me you can do nothing!" We looked at each other, and the words of Jesus challenged and convicted us again about our helplessness and dependence upon Him. Without total, daily reliance on Christ, the study of His Word and being continually in prayer, we can do nothing.

The evidence of this dependence on God is obvious. Life becomes a happy balance of what should be and what actually is. Self-interest diminishes, and life is dominated by allegiance to God, evident to family and friends. Pastors and their wives lead most effectively by example.

What hinders us from loving God with all our being? We need to confess that sin to the Lord and we will be freed from the guilt that takes away our joy (see 1 John 1:9).

Do you desire to be holy and righteous? If you are filled with the Holy Spirit, you will have no room for self-reliance. Your attitude will then be God-centered, your devotion will be to Him. You will be filled with praise and singleness of heart and your dependence will be on Him. You will desire to please God, not to meet the unrealistic expectations of others. You will be relieved of the pressures placed upon you as a pastor's wife.

What about the many demands on my time? Balancing my commitment to the Lord and the responsibilities of the pastorate is the struggle. My husband needs me, the children certainly demand most of my day, I am faced constantly with the hurts and heartaches of the members of our congregation. How can I do it all? Priorities become unclear and are in conflict as pressures mount.

When my husband and I began in this pastorate more than 20 years ago, I was somewhat dismayed. As the wife of an evangelist for the preceding 18 years, I was not responsible to a group of people. Suddenly, I felt pressure I had never felt before. It soon became apparent that former ministers' wives did things a certain way and the hints began.

"Our third minister's wife headed vacation Bible school; our fifth minister's wife taught the junior department; our last minister's wife

"If Daddy is called pastor, what do we call you?" Our children suggested that an appropriate title would be "Mommy Pastor."

had 20 people in her home every Sunday night." Enter stress and uncertainty, and those "people-imposed" boundaries and mandates on my life that you, too, have faced.

Our children began to feel uncertain, too. "If Daddy is called pastor, what do we call you?" One of them suggested that an appropriate title would be "Mommy Pastor." As humorous as that is, we often don't clearly understand our "job description."

A Supportive Husband

We have all had someone say to us, "I wouldn't be a pastor's wife for anything." When my husband and I were called to our first pastorate, I expressed concern to him about my role in the church. What would I do? Where would I fit in? He so wisely said, "Honey, you are the pastor's wife, not the church's wife."

That single statement gave me more freedom than you can imagine. The counsel we had received early in our ministry led us to believe that God comes first, ministry comes second and whatever time is left over is given to family. It is often assumed that pastors must meet the needs of their church members before they respond to their own family's needs. This was never more frustratingly true than on a Christmas morning early in our pastorate. We had just settled in front of our Christmas tree to open presents when the telephone rang. A relative of a church member was desperately in need of help. "Could Ross come immediately?"

The usual discussion ensued, complete with moans and groans from three frustrated children and an unnecessary barb or two from an equally frustrated "mommy pastor." I am not very proud of the fact that I made my husband feel terribly ambivalent and guilty about leaving. But, he returned quickly, having ministered to a person in deep need.

This same struggle would be repeated many times over the next 20 years; but with increased growth and spiritual maturity we all learned how to "present [ourselves] a living [willing] sacrifice," thereby making ourselves "acceptable to God, which is [our] reasonable service" (Rom. 12:1). That's the key—we are servants. Remembering that keeps me from self-pity and refocuses my commitment.

Train Children to Love God

If God has blessed the pastor and his wife with children, the time crunch increases. We have watched some Christian families torn apart by the conflict and frustration of church versus family. We have seen well-meaning pastors' wives giving themselves so enthusiastically to meeting the needs of the congregation that their children were left to manage by themselves. Sometimes rebellion and resentment built against parents. In some cases, bitterness developed and children walked away from the Lord and left the church.

We have learned that we must maintain a proper perspective. As our children grew, the church grew, and the demands on me increased at home and at the church. As I became more uncertain, my husband encouraged me to seek the Lord's wisdom to decide how to divide my time and responsibilities, never pressuring me to be or to do what was "expected."

I am sure most pastors' wives are "expected" at prayer meeting, but many times I sat at one of the children's basketball games instead. Because I loved to play the piano, I enjoyed playing at almost every service, even when we had three morning services before our new sanctuary was built. But it soon became too much, and the children had to wait through extra services. Although they did not complain, I didn't want them to resent Christian service or the church. It was not a difficult decision to cut back on my schedule.

Our prayer, goal and heart's desire has always been 3 John 4: "I have no greater joy than to hear that my children walk in truth."

For the 18 years my husband traveled as an evangelist, it was my joy and responsibility to teach the Scriptures to our children. They remember with mixed feelings the endless charts containing verses and chores for each week. We started in September to learn the Christmas story, Luke 2:1-20, in addition to our weekly verses. Our adult children still grin at Christmastime when Luke 2 is read, as if to say, "We remember when we learned that!" Our children wrote out their verses each weekend on 3x5-inch cards, harder verses for the older ones, easier ones for the younger children. These cards lay on the kitchen table, and it wasn't long before the verses were "absorbed." We used many boxes of colored stars to mark their successes.

Teaching our children the truths in God's Word was a fulfilling experience. As we watched them grow and mature, we saw an increased dependence on God in their lives. Our two sons are ministers who are now teaching others God's wonderful truths, and our daughter and one son are passing along what they have learned to our eight grandchildren.

About eight years ago a second son was born to our son Steve and his wife, Carter. He is a precious, beautiful child who was afflicted with spina bifida. The prognosis was devastating, but after many operations he now walks with a walker. At the time of his birth, we watched Steve and Carter deal with this blow to their young lives. As they applied God's truths and trusted Christ so beautifully, we rejoiced in their maturity. There was no blaming God. Steve said, "Since God is in control of our lives, He could have prevented this. But He didn't. Now let's go on and see how God can mature us and how He can use us to be a witness."

After about six months of waiting on the Lord, Steve said, "If I

God has called pastors' wives to a unique area of service, to His work, in His place, in His time. He will equip us to do the work He has given us to do.

could have a perfect child but had to be where I was spiritually before Benjamin was born, I would rather have Benjamin." At that point, I opened my Bible, pointed to 3 John 4 written in the front and said, "Steve, if Dad and I could have died to have prevented this from happening, we would have done so in a second. You have learned God's truths all your life and have applied them so well. I now want to underline the word "walk" in that verse. This has truly been the greatest joy of my life—to watch you walk what you believe."

Certainly, training our children to love the Lord and walk with Him is of utmost importance, and we thank God that today all three of our children, their spouses and children, love Christ and seek to honor and serve Him in all they do.

I need to emphasize, however, that regardless of how much time and effort a pastor and his wife devote to their children, a child may still go astray. Sincere parenting efforts do not always result in godly, well-behaved, Christian adult children. Pastors' families have many advantages other families do not have, but they do not have a fool-proof edge over other families in raising perfect children.

Jesus Promises Wisdom for the Challenge

We, as pastors' wives, have a huge, wonderful and fulfilling task. God has called us to a unique area of service, to His work, in His place, in His time. He will equip us to do the work He has given us to do. We are God's servants, bought by the sacrifice of His life and blood, and set aside (taken out of this world) and into His service to do His will and work.

We have Jesus' promise in John 10:4: "When he brings out his own sheep, he goes before them; and the sheep follow him, for they know his voice." God has promised you wisdom in every area of your life. "If any of you lacks wisdom, let him ask of God, who gives to all liberally and without reproach, and it will be given to him" (Jas. 1:5). "The Lord gives wisdom; from His mouth come knowledge and understanding" (Prov. 2:6).

Are you daily increasing in the knowledge of God? We are reminded frequently in the Psalms to meditate on God's words. Out of His words come wisdom and understanding. One of my greatest joys is the use of a daily Bible, the *New International Version* or *The Amplified Bible.* My edition dates the pages, and each day gives portions of the Old Testament, New Testament, Psalms and Proverbs. It is helpful to underline, make written comments in the margins and memorize selected Scriptures.

One thing that has kept me focused in my daily Bible reading is the habit of writing down one or two questions to consider. If I read, "I will extol [magnify your name] the Lord at all times; his praise will always be on my lips" (Ps. 34:1, *NIV*), I write on a card: "Do I magnify God's name? Do I always praise or do I complain?" I am then compelled all day to answer these questions, and my life becomes centered on pleasing God.

We are strengthened according to His Word. We will be honest in our speech. The mark of holiness is the Holy Spirit-controlled tongue.

If we are filled with His Word, His wisdom will flow through our tongues. What greater help could there be for a pastor's wife—someone who is always expected to say the right thing at the right time?

The life of the pastor's wife is more difficult than many imagine. Only a woman who is wholly committed to God and the ministry given to her and her husband can possibly cope with the many pressures of that ministry. Few people realize the loneliness, insecurity, struggles and feelings of helplessness when the needs of others and the responsibilities of meeting those needs are so great.

One of the most difficult things I cope with is unjustified criticism against my husband. Much of the criticism is constructive, but mean-spirited jealousies and gossip are unnecessary and wrong. No one but God Himself can comfort us. My husband and I have recently gone through the hardest experience of our lives and have found ourselves standing ALONE but for the mighty, powerful strength of God's arms and promises. Except for the commitment to God that each of us made decades ago and continue to reaffirm every day, we would most certainly give up.

As a pastor's wife, I could not survive without personal commitment and discipline in my spiritual life. The empowerment for all I face comes directly from my Lord, who has called me. "Be strong in the Lord and in the power of His might" (Eph. 6:10). Because I have this strength, I am protected from Satan's attacks of self-pity and discouragement, and will not be demoralized and useless in God's service.

I must depend wholly on God, "praying *always* with *all* prayer and supplication in the Spirit, being watchful to this end with *all* perseverance and supplication for *all* the saints" (Eph. 6:18, italics added).

We cannot be spared those things Jesus suffered as well. But God has called us to walk with Him, to be faithful in service.

In His prayer to the Father, Jesus said, "I have glorified You on the earth. I have finished the work which You have given Me to do" (John 17:4). Jesus' commitment to glorify and obey God and be faithful in God's work sets an example for us to "follow in his steps" (1 Pet. 2:21, *NIV*).

CHAPTER THIRTEEN

The Great Sorority

Lynne Dugan

Victoria, a New Pastor's Wife

Victoria, a new pastor's wife, comes out of a career in high-tech management into another challenging, but entirely different vocation—pastoral ministry. But, having no previous mentors to copy, and lacking pastors' wives to model, she feels lost. So at times she thinks she may be a "little crazy" and feels lonely and isolated. Victoria wishes she could just talk to another female.

Loneliness, a Cause of Stress

Loneliness is no stranger to women in ministry. One of the most significant factors producing stress in this vocation is the lack of friends, because pastors' wives usually have few social outlets to rid themselves of tension. It is rare when ministry wives have close friends inside, or outside, their church. Most common is the conventional wisdom that "everyone knows" pastors' wives should not have personal friends in their church. Back in seminary days, that was the standard message I read in books for women married to ministers. So when problems come, they have no one to turn to for helpful advice. Even though they give their concerns to the Lord, they still feel the need of one or more friends in whom they can confide.

Interdependence Is the Goal

A mental independence tends to build up among ministry women where they have taken on the "do your own thing" mentality. But what is desperately needed is interdependence—to bear each other's burdens, while at the same time nurturing a personal relationship with the Lord, so that He can bear their burden too.

> Two are better than one, because they have a good return for their work: If one falls down, [her] friend can help [her] up. But pity the [woman] who falls and has no one to help [her] up!...Though one may be overpowered, two can defend themselves. A cord of three strands is not quickly broken (Eccles. 4:9,12, *NIV*).

The Importance of Prayer Support

About 30 years ago, a Korean pastor was very sick. Although he had always been a loner, he decided to reach out and ask the men in his church to form small groups that would share and care for each other and pray for his health. When these men refused, he disregarded the Korean culture's typical expectations and went to the women in his small church. They said yes to his request, and formed small groups. As a result, the pastor's health improved, and in time the church had 10,000 support groups, 150,000 members and six services. Now you know "the rest of the story," as Paul Harvey would say, about the famous pastor, David Yonggi Cho, of the Yoido Full Gospel Church in Seoul, Korea.

Isn't it interesting that the first thing our Lord did before He began His ministry was to call 12 men to be His friends, not just His seminary students. Apparently Jesus valued close friends who would experience spiritual community and be answerable to Him and to each other. Jesus prayed that we might be perfected in unity so we would be one as He was with His Father. We can be the answer to Jesus' prayer by coming together to bring about unity among evangelical women. But how can we if we do not make the effort to get together?

The Importance of Support Groups

Support groups have sprouted up spontaneously in the last decade or two for every conceivable category of people—except for pastors' wives. Self-help groups, within and apart from churches, have been providing relationships that offer meaningful community. At least 14 to 16 million Americans belonged to about 500,000 self-help groups in 1990, and the number seems to be doubling every year. The main reasons these groups are so effective is because they provide a sense of belonging, get rid of the feeling of loneliness and resolve many personal problems.

Within the very walls of any church that sponsors self-help groups is often a pastoral family that stands alone without such close ties of friendship. Yet the majority of pastors' wives who took the National Association of Evangelicals' anonymous survey said they needed to be in a support group, but were not. One woman said,

"I'm not finding the friend within or outside my church who I can be with in this pastorate."

Another pastor's wife wrote, "I wish there were support groups for pastors' wives so I'd realize I'm not alone—where I could be myself. We could help one another through difficult situations so we could cope better."

Support groups are a wonderful avenue to encourage and bear up everyone: to bind together those who have common interests.

The doctor's wife, for example, does not know her husband's patients, or if she does, normally it is just a few, and she does not minister to them. The pastoral ministry is unique in that no other professional family lives and works within a larger family—the congregation. Therefore, in order for the pastor's wife to better cope with loneliness and stress, it is imperative for her to find companionship with other ministers' wives. She needs to "take time to smell the flowers"—or to smell each other's perfume!

Nobody understands a pastor's wife better than another pastor's wife. No need for seminars to understand each other! In fact, anyone can be a catalyst to start her own support group of friends. And she might as well realize no one else is likely to do that for her.

Recently, I discovered that the word "religion" is a combination of two Latin words, *re* and *ligare*, and one of the meanings is "to bind together." The "cord" of friendship that binds us together will keep us strong, but if we remain alone we can fall and lie defenseless as the enemy defeats us in ways increasing numbers of pastoral families have experienced, especially in this last decade.

One minister's wife painted a helpful analogy in her letter: she needed a "buddy system." My mind flashed back to a Girl Scout camp when I was learning to swim. How safe and secure I felt having my buddy nearby. That is how women in ministry want to feel: secure in having someone nearby who can keep them from going under.

Geese have a workable buddy system, too. When the lead goose gets tired, it changes places with the one in the wing of the V-formation and another flies point. When one goose gets sick or wounded, two fall out of formation with it and follow it down to help and protect it. They stay with the recovering goose until she is able to fly again.

Support Group for Pastors' Wives

Support groups are a wonderful avenue to encourage and bear up everyone: to bind together those who have common interests. When this desperate need for companionship among ministry women became obvious, we developed the Support Group for Pastors' Wives in the nation's capital, including Maryland and Virginia suburbs. (See appendix 1 for more information about the Support Group for Pastors' Wives.)

Dared to Dream

I dared to dream that women in pastoral ministry would want to form relationships in a safe, nonjudgmental atmosphere where we could let our hair down and be ourselves. The desire was to "have fellowship...with the Father, and with His Son Jesus Christ" (1 John 1:3, *NASB*). And to give "encouragement in Christ,...fellowship of the Spirit,...affection and compassion,...by being of the same mind, maintaining the same love, united in spirit" (Phil. 2:1,2, *NASB*). And I prayed for more than half a year that I would meet other women in church ministry who would share my vision.

Created a Core

God led me to five enthusiastic, committed evangelical ministers' wives who created a core to start our own group; no two women came from the same denomination. Trust grew among us, allowing honest exchange of our feelings—privileges, pleasures, problems and pain. A suffering pastor's wife expressed her sentiments in the NAE survey, "We need support groups to encourage us in this difficult and demanding position. I think many pastors' wives are dying on the vine and no one cares."

The last thing we need to do is feel sorry for ourselves as victims. Instead, let's choose to rejoice in our commitment to serve God our Father. His Son, Jesus Christ, is the vine and we are the branches (see John 15:5). Therefore, we will not "die on the vine" when we abide in Him, although we will be pruned to produce more spiritual fruit. Jesus nourishes us with life and gives us joy as we draw strength from Him in daily prayer and in the living Word of God. We are not the society of the forlorn. We are the sorority of the forgiven.

In the support group, you may choose to remain in a small group or to go another step.

Planned a Program

Our leadership core planned a program determined to reach a wider base of women in the D.C. metro area. We knew we hit a nerve when we read the anonymous feedback sheets from our first retreat:

"I've been looking for a family and now I've found one."

Another ministry woman wrote that she came with a "cold heart, but left with a warm one."

"I feel like I've been acting like an assistant pastor and hadn't intended to. I need to work less and play more so my marriage and ministry will succeed," was another woman's reflection.

As the core group thought things through, we settled on a three-fold purpose.

First, we wanted *to encourage women socially* (see 1 John 1:3,7), primarily affirming them by providing fellowship. A directory, telephone prayer chain, a newsletter—*WOMEN* (Wives Of Ministers

Encouraging Nationally), notebooks containing resources and bibliographies were materials to assist networking and ministry.

One woman spoke for us all: "I can go off duty and relax with everybody."

One ministry woman went home after our retreat and the next day her "church fell apart." She said, "What you shared on the panel that day helped me through the next."

At one of our larger gatherings, I asked the women for a show of hands on how many had a confidante. Only 2 of 50 women raised their hands! After a few more events, the same question was repeated and almost half of the women indicated they now had a close friend. Today, they all say they have personal friends because of their support group.

Second, we wanted *to equip women vocationally* (2 Tim. 3:17), assisting them to reach their fullest potential by providing a variety of programs to be "equipped for every good work." Also, stimulating mentoring is taking place among the young and older, more experienced women. It is encouraging to see this being done naturally now, without having to plan a special seminar on mentoring. The majority of women the NAE surveyed wrote that they thought they could greatly benefit learning from a mentor.

Here are several events we found to be effective:

A seminar for "Couples in Ministry" with the spouses is led by a nationally known Christian counseling clinic, which arranges a tailor-made program for us. Each event is programmed around responses to questionnaires, so they know what needs to address.

On Vision Day, we evaluated our past programs and both dreamed and discussed what we wanted to do in the future. Mary Sue said, "This group helps me maintain my vision. It lets me know there is hope for my ministry. It's encouraging to be replenished each time I come. God is working."

Third, we desired *to edify women spiritually* so that "each of us please [her] neighbor for [her] good, to [her] edification" (Rom. 15:2, *NASB*; cf. 1 Cor. 14:3). We not only meet in the large group in winter, spring and fall, but also join together in monthly, local covenant groups for prayer, Bible study and fellowship. Betty Lou says she rates this as a highlight of her month. "Sharing prayer concerns and helpful Bible study materials I can use in my women's ministries, is a real plus. I wouldn't miss it for the world."

The greatest cause for loneliness is our superhuman expectations of ourselves and others. We need to know we are human—not perfect.

At one of our retreats, Jane confided that when she came to her covenant group she felt comfortable, as if she were "wearing her bedroom slippers" and could "unzip her heart."

Helen, a pastor's wife facing retirement, remarked that the most helpful thing for her has been the nonjudgmental attitudes that encourage a spirit of acceptance. "Although we are different ages, young and older women, and come from different denominations and fellowships, we have real unity in the body. You know, we could be easily wiped out if we had social strata."

The greatest cause for loneliness is our superhuman expectations of ourselves and others. We need to know we are human—not perfect. Sharing our lives and praying for one another removes the temptation to hide behind our masks, and in doing so we discover we are no longer lonely. As we mature in our fellowship with the Lord, deeper relationships naturally develop with our sisters in Christ.

It is exciting to see women exercising their spiritual gifts with each other's women's groups. Martha designed and coordinated a wellness program for a Virginia hospital, so she not only led a "Making Stress Work for You" retreat for our group, but her friend Shirley asked her to do the same program for her church ladies. Then Shirley in turn led worship and sang for Martha's women's retreat a few months later.

Broadened Our Base
We broadened our base and are spawning Support Groups for Pastors' Wives across the nation through the NAE Women's Commission. The commission caught the vision and adopted the same format to promote forming support groups through their denominations.

Victoria Found Her Group

Whatever happened to my friend, Victoria, the new pastor's wife? She will tell you in her own words:

> The support group created a bond where I could say, "That's my group." We have common vision and solutions. You helped me process my feelings and I could walk through the problems. I could get past them because of our core prayer partnership. I don't feel traumatized anymore. Instead, I feel safe—accepted. I realize my problems are common, not unusual in church ministry. I learned from you how to handle tough situations. There are answers. You are my first group outside of John, my husband. You became my family. You can't put a dollar sign on it!

As Support Groups for Pastors' Wives form in every state, we believe they can encourage friendships, help eliminate loneliness and reverse the downward spiral toward burnout so prevalent among ministry wives. By strengthening women in ministry and their families, such groups will enhance the work of thousands of congregations, and eventually the entire Body of Christ.

"The eyes of the Lord move to and fro throughout the earth that He may strongly support those whose heart is completely His" (2 Chron. 16:9, *NASB*).

Am I my sister's keeper? Yes!

ppendices

---

*All appendices material used by permission of the
National Association of Evangelicals.*

*Permission to photocopy the appendices for other than
personal use is prohibited.*

APPENDIX ONE

NAE WOMEN'S COMMISSION
and the TASK FORCE on the FAMILY
SURVEY of MINISTERS' WIVES

Section 1

Following are possible resources for pastors' wives that are either already available or could possibly be made available at a future time. For each resource, please fill in the letter that most closely describes your feelings about that resource.

A —Even if this resource were available, I would not be interested.
B —I would take advantage of this resource if it were available.
C —This resource is already available and satisfactorily meets my needs.

1 ____ National pastors' wives magazine
2 ____ National pastors' wives newsletter
3 ____ National conference for pastors' wives
4 ____ Regional pastors' wives conference
5 ____ National conference for pastors' wives and their husbands to meet personal needs
6 ____ Regional conference for pastors' wives and their husbands to meet personal needs
7 ____ Local pastors' wives support groups
8 ____ Local retreat for pastors' wives

Other resources not mentioned above that I am interested in:

_____

_____

_____

Section 2

Please read each statement below. Indicate the extent to which you agree or disagree with each by filling in the letter in the appropriate column. Your answers are completely anonymous.

A—Strongly disagree   B—Disagree   C—Neutral
D—Agree   E—Strongly agree

1 _____ I feel the congregation gives me the freedom to be myself.
2 _____ I think I am adequately trained for my role.
3 _____ I have difficulty finding time for both family and church ministry.
4 _____ Church ministry is not challenging enough for me.
5 _____ I feel very fulfilled in my role as a pastor's wife.
6 _____ I need more training to be the kind of pastor's wife I'd like   to be.
7 _____ I feel as if the congregation puts me on a pedestal.
8 _____ Being a pastor's wife is better than I had hoped.
9 _____ I feel that the ministry is God's will for my life as well as for my husband's.
10 _____ I would be glad if we could drop out of the ministry.
11 _____ My role is no different than that of most wives in our church.
12 _____ Sometimes I feel like a yo-yo with frequent up and down emotions about myself.
13 _____ I feel confident in my role as a pastor's wife.
14 _____ I love being a pastor's wife and can't think of anything else   I'd rather be.
15 _____ I feel as if I'm on a treadmill and can't get off.
16 _____ I think my husband's ministry is definitely appreciated by the church.

17 _____ The people in our church don't really understand me.

18 _____ The church apparently thinks it hired me to be an unpaid assistant pastor.

19 _____ I feel like I am close to burnout because of the demands I face as a pastor's wife.

20 _____ I do not have enough influence in my church.

21 _____ I often struggle with feelings of anger and bitterness.

22 _____ I only attend church services and accept no other responsibilities in our church.

23 _____ There are no other women in our church adequately trained to work with me.

24 _____ People in the church assume that I know the Bible well, but I don't.

For me, the most fulfilling part of being a pastor's wife is

_____

_____

_____

The most frustrating thing about my role as a minister's wife is

_____

_____

_____

I feel I could be a better pastor's wife if

_____

_____

_____

On a scale from A to E, how well does each word or phrase below describe your role as a pastor's wife?

Not at all   Perfectly
        A   B   C   D   E

1 _____ Rewarding
2 _____ Lonely
3 _____ Challenging
4 _____ Unnerving

5 _____ Exciting
6 _____ Frustrating
7 _____ Stressful
8 _____ Satisfying
9 _____ Educational
10 _____ Routine
11 _____ Demanding
12 _____ Self-revealing
13 _____ Confining
14 _____ Humbling
15 _____ Skill-developing
16 _____ Hurtful
17 _____ Exhausting
18 _____ Stretching
19 _____ Frightening
20 _____ Depressing

My current responsibilities in the church are

_____

_____

_____

If I were a denominational leader with an awareness of pastors' wives needs, I would

_____

_____

_____

One thing seminaries could do to better prepare pastors' wives is

_____

_____

_____

Section 3: Spiritual Life

1   In the past week, how many days did you set aside some time for personal Bible study and prayer?

None   1   2 or 3   4 or 5   6 or 7

2   Which of the following best describes your relationship with
    Jesus Christ at this time?

    _____   Developing steadily
    _____   Stable and satisfying
    _____   Stable, but not wholly satisfying
    _____   Becoming less important
    _____   I'm not sure I know Jesus Christ personally

Why did you answer Question 2 as you did?

_____
_____
_____

3   On a scale from A to E, how do you think God views you
    right now?

Disappointed   Pleased
            A   B   C   D   E

Section 4

Following are several problems families face today in our society.
Please circle those concerns which you personally have dealt with in
your own family in the last 12 months.

1   Drugs
2   Alcohol
3   Premarital sex
4   Homosexuality
5   Child abuse
6   Wife abuse
7   Incest
8   Pornography

Please read each statement and indicate the extent to which you
agree or disagree with each by filling in the letter in the appropriate

column. Again, your answers are completely anonymous.

A—Strongly disagree B—Disagree   C—Neutral
D—Agree   E—Strongly agree

9 ____ My husband and I have a healthy, compatible marriage.
10 ____ Our children seem to like being the children of a minister.
11 ____ I am frightened because my husband is closer to some women in the church than he is to me.
12 ____ I have no close personal friends in our church because I must not show favoritism.
13 ____ Our children are causing us real concern right now.
14 ____ My husband has no personal friends who can serve as a support to him.
15 ____ There are people in our church whom I will never be able to forgive.
16 ____ If we didn't have to hold our marriage together because of the church or for our children, I would consider divorce.
17 ____ I have absolute confidence that my husband would never become interested in another woman.

On a scale from A to E, indicate to what extent each is a present concern in your marriage.

Serious concern   Not a concern
     A   B   C   D   E

18 ____ Moving from one pastorate to another
19 ____ My own lack of full commitment to my husband's ministry
20 ____ Competing with the congregation's demands on my husband
21 ____ Lack of communication between my husband and me
22 ____ My emotional needs not being met by my husband
23 ____ Feelings of guilt because I want more time with my husband

24 ____ Fears about my husband's counseling with women
25 ____ My own thoughts about a relationship with someone other than my husband
26 ____ Feel disqualified for the ministry because of unresolved marital problems

Other areas of concern I face are

_____
_____
_____
_____
_____

Following are several common needs among pastors' wives. On a scale from A to E, show to what extent each phrase describes a need you are presently feeling in your life.

Serious need   Not a need
     A   B   C   D   E

27 ____ Rest and relaxation
28 ____ Regular exercise
29 ____ A support group I can share and pray with
30 ____ A real vacation
31 ____ Better sexual relationship with my husband
32 ____ A trusted friend I can confide in and have fun with
33 ____ Adequate time with my husband
34 ____ A scheduled day each week we can be together as a family
35 ____ Personal spiritual renewal
36 ____ Emotional healing from past or present painful situation

Other areas of need I face are

_____
_____
_____

Section 5: Life Issues.
On a scale from A to E, indicate the extent to which you have this concern and would like to learn more about possible answers and solutions.

Definite help needed   No help needed
A   B   C   D   E

1 ____ Balancing church responsibilities and family
2 ____ Overcoming guilt feelings
3 ____ Building my self-confidence
4 ____ Overcoming discouragement or depression
5 ____ Handling personal finances better
6 ____ Coping with stress
7 ____ Developing a deeper relationship with God
8 ____ Improving my marriage
9 ____ Discovering and using my spiritual gifts
10 ____ Dealing with discipline problems in our family
11 ____ Controlling my weight
12 ____ Developing counseling skills
13 ____ Developing leadership skills
14 ____ Managing my emotions
15 ____ Learning how to disciple other women
16 ____ Getting more done in the time I have
17 ____ Coping with midlife issues
18 ____ Increasing my Bible knowledge
19 ____ Understanding and relating to our teenagers
20 ____ Preparing for retirement

Other issues of concern to me are

_____
_____
_____
_____
_____
_____

Section 6

Finally, some information about you and your church.

1   How long have you been a pastor's wife?
>   0-5 years
>   6-10 years
>   11-15 years
>   16-20 years
>   21 years and over

2   How long have you been in your present church?
>   0-5 years
>   6-10 years
>   11-15 years
>   16-20 years
>   21 years and over

3   What is the approximate size of your church in the morning worship service?
>   under 100
>   100-249
>   250-349
>   350-499
>   500 or more

4   In what type of area is your church located?
>   city of 100,000 or more
>   city/suburb 25,000-99,999
>   suburb under 25,000
>   own under 25,000
>   rural community

5   Are you a full-time homemaker?
>   Yes   No

6   Do you have children living at home?
>   Yes   No

If YES, how many are in each of the following categories?

7   Under 5 years   _____

8   5 to 11 years   _____
9   12 to 13 years   _____
10   14 to 18 years   _____
11   19 to 23 years   _____
12   24 years or older   _____

What is the title of your husband's current position?

_____

_____

What is the full name of your denomination or association?

_____

13   Do you have a background in a parachurch organization?
         Yes   No
Which parachurch organization(s) do you have a background in?

_____

_____

_____

14   What is your racial or ethnic background?
         Black   White   Hispanic   Oriental   Other
15   Do you have a part-time paid job?
         Yes   No
16   Do you have a full-time paid job?
         Yes   No

If YES, please circle the category.

17   Church ministry
18   Education
19   Business
20   Counseling
21   Nursing
22   Retail sales
23   Secretary
24   Self-employment
25   Writing

OTHER:

_____

_____

_____

Please circle your highest education level.

26   Not a high school graduate
27   High school graduate
28   Technical or business school
29   Bible school (non-degree)
30   Some college or university
31   Undergraduate work
32   Some graduate work
33   Graduate or post-graduate degree
34   What is your age?
          up to 29 years
          30-39 years
          40-49 years
          50-59 years
          60 or more years

APPENDIX TWO

NATIONAL ASSOCIATION of EVANGELICALS
SURVEY of MINISTERS' WIVES
EXECUTIVE SUMMARY

Authored by Lynne Dugan
National Association
of Evangelicals
Women's Commission, 1989

Kenneth E. Crow, Ph.D.
Department of Sociology
MidAmerica Nazarene College
February 1990

NATIONAL ASSOCIATION OF EVANGELICALS
TASK FORCE ON THE FAMILY/WOMEN'S COMMISSION
SURVEY OF MINISTERS' WIVES

Kenneth E. Crow, Ph.D.

The spouse of a minister strongly influences, and is strongly influenced by, her mate's ministry. Consequently, the role that accompanies this relationship seems more demanding and more important than the spouse's role in most other professions. Yet formal training and special resources for this role are relatively rare. Also relatively rare are studies that examine the needs of the wives of clergymen.

Convinced that understanding this role more thoroughly would help both denominations and churches, the National Association of Evangelicals conducted a survey of pastors' wives in the fall of 1989. While the association has in its fellowship churches and denominations that have different views regarding the ordination of women, the overwhelming majority of ministers are men, and therefore, the survey was addressed particularly to their wives. This report summarizes the findings of that study.

The overall pattern found in the study of pastors' wives was quite positive. Large majorities say they enjoy the role. They are fulfilled; they feel adequate for the responsibilities placed upon them; their family life is positive. The role may be more demanding than others, but, the overall picture is of women who are challenged by those demands.

Yet two factors suggest that the positive experience is not universal. Indeed, since the nature of the role may tend to mask problems, some negative aspects of the role may be more extensive than the survey indicates. The role seems to require an optimistic, positive attitude; negative thinking is discouraged. This attitude may be reflected in the responses. A second factor is ministerial attrition. Pastors whose wives feel negatively toward their role may experience difficulty finding and keeping a church. Furthermore, severe family problems often disqualify a pastor. Therefore, the relatively small portion (3 percent) who would consider divorce, for example, may be both an indication of the extent of severe family problems as well as an indication that ministers and wives experiencing such problems may have already left the ministry.

Problems with the role of being a pastor's wife seem to decrease as one grows older. This may be due to those who have worked through unrealistic expectations, adjusting to any discrepancy between their aspirations and the reality they have found in the church. Others may have gained skills through their experiences, resulting in more satisfactory performance and confidence. A less positive explanation for this tendency may be the withdrawal of those who have suffered. In other words, older, more experienced women may tend to be more positive because those who do not find a satisfying niche may influence their husbands to leave the profession.

BASIC FINDINGS

The typical spouse responding to the survey was in her thirties (32 percent) or forties (30 percent). Most (68 percent) had at least one child living at home. Nearly half (45 percent) had completed at least a college education; some (13 percent) had earned a graduate degree.

Slightly more than half (51 percent) considered themselves full-time homemakers, although more than a third (39 percent) were employed part-time. Only 21 percent were employed full-time, the most common occupations being teaching, secretarial, and church ministry. Of the women with preschool children, only 11 percent were employed full-time.

More than half (51 percent) were married to husbands who had been in the ministry more than fifteen years. Almost one-third (33 percent) had been in that role for more than twenty years. Most (58 percent) had been in their present congregations five years or less; only 2 percent had been in their current churches more than twenty years.

Attendance at Sunday morning worship at the churches their husbands pastor was less than 250 people for three-fourths (76 percent). One third (35 percent) served in churches that attract less than one hundred people on Sunday morning.

Respondents identified their churches with fifty-six known denominational groups, as the table on pages 168 to 170 illustrates. While 7 percent of the women claimed to be nondenominational or in churches in unidentifiable fellowships, the highest representation came from denominations in the Baptist tradition (22 percent); the Methodist and holiness tradition (21 percent); and the Continental Anabaptist and pietist tradition (19 percent). Churches in the Presbyterian, Reformed, and Congregational communions accounted for

16 percent while Pentecostal churches accounted for 10 percent. The highest single denominations represented were Southern Baptist (9.7 percent); Assemblies of God (6.3 percent); Church of the Nazarene (7.4 percent); Presbyterian Church, USA (5.9 percent); and Evangelical Free (5.8 percent).

Thirty of the forty-four NAE aligned denominations were represented in the survey, accounting for 50 percent of the respondents. No significant differences were found between the wives of ministers that serve in NAE aligned denominations and the wives of ministers in other denominations or fellowships.

Congregations tended to be in smaller communities. Only one in five respondents (20 percent) lived in a city of 100,000 or more people. One-fourth (24 percent) lived in rural communities and another fourth (26 percent) resided in towns with less than 25,000 people.

Personal Fulfillment
Four out of five (78 percent) wives see their role as God's will for their lives. They believe their husbands' ministries are appreciated (70 percent). Three out of five (60 percent) say they are very fulfilled in the role. Half (51 percent) say they love being married to a clergyman.

Slightly more than half (52 percent) feel they have been adequately trained for the role. This positive evaluation was somewhat more likely for the older, better educated women.

More than three-fourths (77 percent) say their congregations give them freedom to be themselves. Only 4 percent say they refuse to accept any church responsibilities. However, one in five (21 percent) believes parishioners view her as something like an unpaid assistant minister. About the same portion (20 percent) think that most church members do not understand them.

While three out of five (57 percent) feel confident in the role, two out of five (42 percent) say it is difficult to find time for both family and ministry. About the same proportion (41 percent) experience frequent emotional ups and downs. One in six (17 percent) says she is close to burnout.

Adjectives most likely to be selected as strongly characterizing their role were positive descriptions like "challenging" (72 percent); "satisfying" (67 percent); "demanding" (66 percent); "rewarding" (66 percent); and "stretching" (63 percent). Negative possibilities such as "routine" (18 percent), "frightening" (20 percent), and "depressing" (20 percent), were least likely to be chosen.

Respondents were more likely to describe their role as satisfying, the larger the congregation their spouses served. Wives in churches with more than one hundred worshippers were more likely to describe their role as rewarding; wives in churches of less than one hundred worshippers were more inclined to describe their role as depressing.

Younger spouses and especially those with children at home were significantly more likely to describe the role as stressful, hurtful, and frustrating.

Personal and Family Relationships
A large majority (85 percent) of the women say their marriages are healthy and compatible. Four out of five (81 percent) have confidence in their husbands' fidelity. Almost two-thirds (64 percent) say their children enjoy being ministers' kids.

A very small minority (3 percent) say they would consider divorce if it were not for the congregation or the children. A similarly small group (4 percent) claim their husbands are closer to some women parishioners than to themselves or fear their husbands counseling women. Only 3 percent expressed problems with extramarital affairs of their own. Few feel disqualified from the ministry because of marital problems (5 percent). As noted above, the probable time between development of serious marital problems and the withdrawal from the pastoral profession may keep such proportions quite small.

Personal and Spiritual Needs
Three out of five wives (63 percent) say they could use regular exercise. Nearly as many (56 percent) could use some rest and relaxation; nearly half (46 percent) need a "real vacation." Many (44 percent) need a trusted friend. Almost as many would like a support group (41 percent). Two out of five (38 percent) expressed a need

for adequate time with their spouses. Many (38 percent) could use a scheduled day each week devoted to the family.

Developing a deeper relationship with God (55 percent) and spiritual renewal (46 percent) are current needs of most of the women. Half (52 percent) want to increase their Bible knowledge. They evidently experienced some conflict between these desires and the demands of their role. While three out of ten (29 percent) find time for Bible study and personal prayer six or seven days a week, these tend to be the older women and those without children at home. A daily devotional time was not a reality for the majority. Still, most (68 percent) described their relationship with Jesus Christ as developing steadily or as stable and satisfying.

Perceived Ministry Needs
The areas where the highest proportion of pastors' wives feel a need for better ministry skills are: developing counseling skills (57 percent); learning to disciple other women (57 percent); and time management (50 percent). As age and, presumably, experience increased, the proportions indicating a need for those skills decreased somewhat. However, even for those in their sixties, a rather large portion expressed a need for help with such skills.

In family areas, many respondents would like help with understanding and relating to teenagers (35 percent) and balancing the demands of church and family (28 percent). As might be expected, balancing these responsibilities was more of a problem for women under forty than for older ones.

On a personal level, the wives felt the need for help in several areas: coping with stress (52 percent); preparing for retirement (46 percent); controlling one's weight (42 percent); building self-confidence (39 percent); and overcoming discouragement or depression (35 percent). A significantly higher portion of wives with children at home indicated a need for help in coping with stress. The need for help in preparing for retirement tended to increase with age.

The need for help in overcoming depression or discouragement was linked to the number of worshippers in the churches their husbands pastored. While nearly one in five spouses whose husband pastored a larger church needed help in this area, that portion more than doubled for wives whose mates served in smaller congregations. Evidently the tendency to associate ministerial success with congregational size tends to influence a wife's sense of worth.

SURVEY METHODOLOGY

The National Association of Evangelicals selected a manageable sample as a starting point. With no access to a complete list of spouses of clergymen who serve in NAE aligned denominations and churches, the association opted to use the slightly more than 34,000 pastors and churches on its general mailing list. These pastors and churches may or may not hold official NAE membership, have corresponded at some point with NAE, or subscribe to NAE literature. From this list every eleventh name was selected to create a systematic sample of slightly more than three thousand names.

Since the sample was composed of names of churches or clergymen, the questionnaires were sent indirectly to spouses. Ministers or church secretaries were asked to hand the questionnaire to the wife of the pastor. Some ministers and secretaries undoubtedly neglected to do this. Furthermore, many evangelical ministers tend to move to new assignments often, leaving an undetermined number of churches with no pastor when the survey arrived in the mail. Because of these factors, to determine precisely how many wives actually received the questionnaire is virtually impossible. Of the women who did receive the questionnaire, 570 responded.

The size of the response, combined with the nature of the original list, suggests that the research is probably best understood as a pilot study. Like any survey, caution is needed in interpreting the data. Variation due to sampling error might be expected to be as much as 4 percentage points above or below these proportions in a sample this size. Therefore, without additional research, general assertions regarding all wives of evangelical clergymen should be somewhat tentative.

For those who wish to explore specific issues in depth, an

expanded booklet containing tables illustrating extensive information from the total group as well as from selected subgroups is available at a cost of $10.00 postage paid from the National Association of Evangelicals. The tables facilitate comparison of responses by age, education, employment status, the tenure of their husbands' pastorate, number of Sunday worshippers in their church; and the presence of children at home.

CONCLUSIONS AND RECOMMENDATIONS

In addition to providing insights for further research, the National Association of Evangelicals survey enhances contemporary understanding of women who are married to men in the ministry. Wives will find comfort as they discover that their experience is not as isolated as it may have seemed. Denominational leaders will find practical ways they can more effectively assist the mates of those who lead their congregations. Local congregations will learn of ways they can ease the load and help spouses find fulfillment.

In sifting through the data, four basic conclusions emerge that should not only grab the attention of the evangelical community but lead denominations and churches into new avenues of care and concern for the wives of ministers:

1. Training and education are needed, especially for younger wives, in such areas as counseling, discipling tools and techniques, and time management.

2. While the number of clerical marriages experiencing severe problems appears to be relatively small, pastors and their spouses are not immune from the problems that affect other couples. About one in every twenty-five ministers' wives seems to be experiencing severe problems. More important, the expectations placed upon them—combined with the influence they exert on their husbands' effectiveness—may limit the resources available to these women. They may be more isolated from trustworthy and confidential help than other professional wives would be.

3. The wives of ministers share the common needs of busy Amer-

icans. They need help in such areas as coping with stress and preparing for retirement. They need more rest and relaxation than they are getting; a real vacation would be most helpful. While these needs are not unique, the nature of the role may make it even more difficult than usual to respond to them. Clergy salaries and congregational and/or denominational expectations undoubtedly contribute to these problems, rather than their solutions, at least some of the time.

4. Denominations wishing to respond with resources will find the suggestions expressed in the survey helpful. The questionnaire listed several possible resources: a national ministers' wives magazine or newsletter; a national or regional conference for ministers' wives; a national or regional conference for both husbands and wives to meet personal needs; a local support group of pastors' wives; and a local retreat for wives.

None of these resources was perceived to be already available to more than one in five wives. Resource availability ranked in order were local retreat (20 percent); husband and wife regional conference (19 percent); magazine (15 percent); local support group (14 percent); regional conference (13 percent); husband and wife national conference (11 percent); national conference (6 percent); and newsletter (3 percent).

The resources most likely selected as something the women could benefit from were the newsletter (64 percent); the local wives support group (58 percent); and the magazine (56 percent). The resources least selected were the national conference for wives (22 percent) or for husbands and wives (28 percent).

Number of Respondents by Denominational Design
(* *designates NAE aligned denominations*)

Known denominational groups

6   Advent Christian Conference*
3   American Baptist Churches USA

34	Assemblies of God*
8	"Baptist"
1	Baptist Bible Fellowship
24	Baptist General Conference*
1	Bible Fellowship Church
7	Brethren Church*
2	Brethren in Christ Church*
29	Christian and Missionary Alliance*
1	Christian Churches and Churches of Christ
4	Christian Reformed Church*
3	Churches of Christ
1	Church of Christ (Disciples)
3	Church of God
17	Church of God, Anderson, Indiana
1	Church of God, Cleveland, Tennessee*
2	Church of the Lutheran Brethren in America
40	Church of the Nazarene*
2	Church of the United Brethren in Christ*
25	Conservative Baptist Association
10	Conservative Congregational Christian Conference*
1	Elim Fellowship*
2	Episcopal Church
6	Evangelical Church of North America*
7	Evangelical Congregational Church*
13	Evangelical Covenant Church
31	Evangelical Free Church of America*
2	Evangelical Friends Alliance*
4	Evangelical Lutheran Church in America
1	Evangelical Mennonite Church*
3	Evangelical Methodist Church*
4	Evangelical Presbyterian Church*
1	Fellowship of Grace Brethren Churches
15	Free Methodist Church*
3	"Friends"
2	General Association of Regular Baptist Churches
3	General Conference of Mennonite Brethren Churches*

1	Grace Gospel Fellowship
5	International Church of the Foursquare Gospel*
1	Lutheran Church, Missouri Synod
6	Missionary Church*
2	North American Baptist Conference*
5	Open Bible Standard Churches*
3	Orthodox Presbyterian Church
2	Pentecostal Church of God*
2	Pentecostal Holiness Church International*
1	Pillar of Fire
6	"Presbyterian"
14	Presbyterian Church in America*
32	Presbyterian Church, USA
1	Primitive Methodist Church*
6	Reformed Church in America
1	Reformed Episcopal Church
3	Reformed Presbyterian Church of North America*
52	Southern Baptist Convention
2	United Church of Christ
8	United Methodist Church
26	Wesleyan Church*

Nondenominational or unidentifiable groups

1	Bethlehem Congregational
2	Bible Church
1	Bread of Life
1	Catholic
1	Chadburn Gospel Mission
1	Church of God Fellowship
1	Church of God Reformed
1	Faith in Christ Fellowship
28	Nondenominational

APPENDIX THREE

SUPPORT GROUPS for PASTORS' WIVES

*The Steps of a Good Woman Are Ordered by the Lord
Psalm Thirty-seven, Verse Twenty-three*

DARE TO DREAM

of **Assisting** women in reaching their fullest potential through developing relationships with the Lord and Pastors' wives
of **Acknowledging** that pastors' wives have unique needs, and need to cultivate friendships in a safe atmosphere of a peer support group to enhance personal growth/spiritual maturity
of **Affirming** your belief that every woman is created in the image of God, is loved by God and is to be loved by others

We can **Assist** by **Responding** with eagerness, consideration, and courtesy to each woman in ministry
    Resolving to serve the Lord Jesus Christ together
    Respecting all ages, races, and nationalities

We can **Acknowledge** by **Deepening** spiritual insight
    Discovering personal acceptance
    Developing prayer support

We can **Affirm** by **Committing** time to each other
   Caring for each other's needs
   Cultivating spiritual gifts

CREATE A CORE

by **Inviting** pastors' wives to join in the leadership
by **Initiating** trust among core members in honest sharing
by **Inspiring** the core leadership to share your vision

Invite by **Listening** for enthusiastic response
   by **Learning** what needs are to be prayed
   by **Leading** in hospitality

Initiate by **Encouraging** transparency
   by **Enriching** in sharing joys/pains
   by **Enhancing** self-worth of pastors' wives

Inspire by **Sharing** ideas; problem-solving
   by **Shaping** purpose, goals and aims
   by **Structuring** mission and vision statements

PLAN A PROGRAM

to **Encourage** pastors' wives **Socially** in nonjudgmental
  atmosphere to allow interaction which rids loneliness,
  isolation and stress
to **Equip** pastors' wives **Vocationally** by sharing learning skills
to **Edify** pastors' wives **Spiritually**

Encourage by **Providing** inspirational newsletter,
directory,
   by **Praying** using telephone prayer chain, one-on-one,
   table prayer
   by **Planning** one-on-one lunch/sharing babysitting/
   couples get-together

Equip by **Encouraging** mentoring young with older women
>   by **Exchanging** materials for ministry and family
>   by **Enriching** through clinics, retreats, seminars

Edifying by **Empowering** with personal testimonies
>   by **Exercising** spiritual gifts together in ministry
>   by **Encouraging** monthly small prayer groups

FOUR ELEMENTS SUGGESTED for EACH PROGRAM

Plan methods to know each other better.
Pray and worship together.
Participate in small and large groups/feedback sheets or questionnaires.
Promote challenges/commitment to God, each other, and to their ministries

BROADEN THE BASE

>   by **Spawning SUPPORT GROUPS for PASTORS' WIVES (SGPW)** through **NAE Women's Commission**
>   by **Stimulating SGPW** among pastors' wives, denominations, independent fellowships, seminaries
>   by **Spreading** the vision to other communities, districts, and states

Spawn by **Formatting** similar program
>   by **Forming** support groups transdenominationally
>   by **Formulating** strong future support systems

Stimulating by **Ordering** *MINISTRY GUIDES*
>   by **Organizing** "how-to-start" SGPW seminars
>   by **Opening doors** to spread SGPW vision

Spread by **Writing** articles about **SGPW**
by **Working** with **Women's Commission** project
by **Witnessing** about the benefits of **SGPW**

APPENDIX FOUR

THE DC METRO ASSOCIATION
of
EVANGELICAL PASTORS' WIVES

Mission Statement

The DC Metro Association of Evangelical Pastors' Wives is a newly-formed Support Group that links wives of pastors together for mutual encouragement in life and ministry.

This is a fellowship of prayer, hope, and love. We use biblical principles as our basis for building a positive Christian Support Group. This association is committed to provide activities and programs in such a way as to:

- *Assist women in reaching their fullest potential by developing relationships, deepening spiritual insight and understanding.*
- *Acknowledge the unique needs of pastors' wives by cultivating friendships in a safe atmosphere that will enhance personal and professional growth.*
- *Affirm the belief that every woman is a unique individual, created in the image of God, and is to be loved and respected.*

We respond to all wives of pastors with eagerness, consideration, cour-

tesy, and our desire to serve the Lord, respecting all ages, races, and nationalities.

Our fellowship desires each woman the freedom to be truly herself and to appreciate her unique abilities. These goals are attained through a formula of:

Acceptance, Affection, Affirmation, Discovery, Commitment, Prayer, Reward, Recognition, and Reinforcement.

The DC Metro Association of Evangelical Pastors' Wives is a ministry initiated in the nation's capital by the Task Force on the Family of the National Association of Evangelicals. For more information please contact the National Association of Evangelicals (NAE) at: 1023 15th Street, N.W. Suite 500, Washington, DC 20005 (202/789-1011)

APPENDIX FIVE

THE DC METRO ASSOCIATION of EVANGELICAL PASTORS' WIVES SUPPORT GROUP

THE NATIONAL ASSOCIATION of EVANGELICALS STATEMENT of FAITH

1. We believe the Bible to be the inspired, the only infallible, authoritative Word of God.
2. We believe that there is one God, eternally existent in three persons: Father, Son and Holy Spirit.
3. We believe in the deity of our Lord Jesus Christ, in His virgin birth, in His sinless life, in His miracles, in His vicarious and atoning death through His shed blood, in His personal return to power and glory.
4. We believe that for salvation of lost and sinful man, regeneration by the Holy Spirit is absolutely essential.
5. We believe in the present ministry of the Holy Spirit by whose indwelling the Christian is enabled to live a godly life.
6. We believe in the resurrection of both the saved and the lost; they that are saved unto the resurrection of life and they that are lost unto the resurrection of damnation.

7. We believe in the spiritual unity of believers in our Lord
    Jesus Christ.

SIGNATURE OF DCMAEPW CORE MEMBER   DATE

Member of Support Groups for Pastors' Wives
1023 15th Street, NW, Suite 500
Washington, DC 20005
202/789-1011

Support Groups for Pastors' Wives

Want more information?
Use the form below to request brochures, Tables of the NAE Survey or the Ministry Guide. The Ministry Guide includes a complete mission statement, suggested activities, list of qualified resource persons, a bibliography of books, newsletters and other materials.

Please mail your order prepaid to:

Mrs. Lynne Dugan
1023 15th Street N.W. Suite 500
Washington, DC 20005
(202) 789-1011

Name_____

Title_____

Organization_____

Street/Box#_____

City_____ State_____ Zip_____

Phone (___) _____

Quantity	Price	Total
_____ Ministry Guides	@ $5.00	$_____
_____ "Support Groups for Pastors' Wives" brochures		$_____
Up to 100 15¢ each		
100-500 10¢ each		
_____ Tables of NAE Survey	@$10.00	$_____
Please add 20% shipping cost		$_____
Total fund enclosed		$_____

NOTE: If you, or anyone you know, have started a support group for pastors' wives, Lynne Dugan would like to hear from you. Please write to her at the NAE office.